THE GREEN DUMB

Guide to Houseplants

45 Unfussy Plants That Are Easy to Grow and Hard to Kill

Holly Theisen-Jones

CHRONICLE BOOKS

SAN FRANCISCO

Library of Congress Cataloging-in-Publication Data available.

ISBN 978-1-7972-1664-5
Manufactured in China.

Designed by Maggie Edelman.
Illustrations by Lucila Perini.

10 9 8 7 6 5 4 3 2

Chronicle Books LLC
680 Second Street
San Francisco, California 94107
www.chroniclebooks.com

Dedicated to The Egg.

Contents

Acknowledgments

I could never have written this book without the support of my husband, Michael Theisen-Jones, who kept all the plates spinning and all the outdoor plants alive. Thank you for believing in me and insisting I keep going, even when our many projects and obligations collided with one another. I also owe a huge debt of gratitude to my sister, Andy Jones, my mother, Betsy Duggan, and Kelsey Fredriksen, all generous and talented writers whose feedback and support shaped this book and kept me sane. Special thanks as well to my father, Ezra Jones, for your boundless enthusiasm and free legal advice. Without all of your reality checks, encouragement, and indispensable help, I'd still be chewing on a ballpoint pen and staring at a blank Word document.

I'm extremely grateful to Jamie Thompson at Chronicle Books for reading my short humor pieces and believing I had a book in me. Enormous thanks for your guidance, insight, and support through this entire process! I also want to thank Chris Monks at McSweeney's Internet Tendency for opening the door for me to share my writing and Irving Ruan for great feedback, encouragement, and laughing at my jokes.

I deeply appreciate the many professors, horticulturists, master gardeners, and other professionals and volunteers who share their expertise and passion for plants through extension programs across the United States. I'd especially like to thank Susan and Dan Mahr of the University of Wisconsin, Leonard Perry of the University of Vermont, Karen Russ and Al Pertuit of Clemson University, Emma Erler of the University of New Hampshire, Gerald Klingaman of the University of Arkansas, and the faculty and master gardeners at the University of

Florida Institute of Food and Agricultural Sciences and North Carolina State University for creating such high-quality, accessible resources.

Finally, I'd like to thank Paul Blackmore at the Atlanta Botanical Garden for teaching me everything I know about keeping tropical plants alive.

Introduction

Do you wish you could have cool plants, even though you're a hot mess? Never fear. Nature is several steps ahead of you.

A few years ago, I thought I had found my dream job in a tropical greenhouse. As it turns out, wanting to be surrounded by plants and having the skill to keep them alive are completely separate things. Two slipped discs and a hundred dead specimens later, I called it quits, but my home has remained a tiny, cluttered jungle of plant experiments ever since.

I'll be honest with you: I have a brown thumb. If the publisher had asked me to provide photographs of my own plants, this book would not exist. If plant murder were a crime, I'd be hiding in Central America under a fake name. A lot of my experiments fail. When I succeed, though, the thrill of seeing a bright green NEW BABY LEAF is wholesome and satisfying. I want you to experience it, too.

That said, reader, beware. Plants are addictive. Every food-safe container that passes through my kitchen goes on to house a seedling or a cutting. My dining table is a potting table. I hoard seedling mix the way people hoarded toilet paper at the beginning of the COVID-19 pandemic. While it is possible to have just a few houseplants like a normal person, you could also hit "moss bottom." You've been warned.

Why Bother?

If you've picked up this book, you might be having mixed feelings about going back to a plant nursery or garden center to recruit new victims. Maybe you've stood by helplessly as a cactus turned to slime, or you've endured the perpetual indoor autumn of an unhappy ficus. I encourage you to try again for several reasons.

First, plants are good for your health. They give off oxygen and improve indoor air quality. Some houseplants can remove allergens and scavenge the volatile organic compounds spewed by office appliances. It might not be enough to treat your asthma, but it could be enough to convince your spouse to spring for the big philodendron when all you really needed from Home Depot was a putty knife.

Plants are also great for your mental health. Simply being around plants has a relaxing effect on people. Studies indicate marked improvements in mood, task performance, and stress biomarkers. Studies show that even fake plants are beneficial to our well-being. They show that just looking at the color green benefits our well-being. Looking at *literally anything other than a phone* benefits our well-being.

Plants make great pets and roommates. No peace lily will ever criticize you for quitting your workout video to go finish a box of Triscuits. There are no poop bags or litter boxes to deal with, and if your clinical depression comes raging back, plant neglect is not a reportable offense. Houseplants offer quiet company and no judgment.

Finally, plants add a touch of charm and whimsy to any space. Does your bedroom have a mattress on the floor and Christmas lights taped to the wall? Put a money tree in the corner. Instant upgrade! Are you a corporate lackey trapped under fluorescent lights and a drop-tile ceiling? A colorful calathea or a chunky little aloe could help restore your will to live. Of course, it's best if they're not turning to sludge and drawing ants. That's where this book comes in.

All of the plants in this book have two things in common: They're easy to find and hard to kill. Some of them have absurd backstories from the Victorian heyday that brought them into the horticultural trade. Get ready to judge your houseguests based on their reactions to botanical trivia! Others have unexpected ethnobotanical uses, but beyond the herbs, don't plan on eating anything in this book. I don't want the lawsuit, and you don't want the diarrhea and heart palpitations. Whether you're looking for a plant that's so easy it could be plastic (ZZ plants) or something slightly more ambitious (monstera), the information here will help you get started.

The Unavoidable Basics

The main ingredients for houseplant survival are water, light, containers, and soil. Let's examine each one in more detail.

Water

While plenty of plants perish from neglect and dryness, overwatering is the leading cause of houseplant death (if you were trapped up to the waist in murky water, you'd turn yellow too). The secret to watering houseplants is not to make *watering* a habit, but *checking the soil* to see whether the top few inches are dry. With a modicum of attention and willingness to touch dirt, you can manage this. If it's dust all the way down, up your watering game. If it's swampy even days after you last watered, back off. I personally like to check and water my plants while brewing my coffee: Everybody in the household, human or herbaceous, gets their survival juice at the same time. It's only fair. Keeping a cute, small watering can close to the coffee maker is a handy reminder.

Unless specific instructions say otherwise, most plants in this book like their soil to dry at least partially, if not completely, between waterings. I call this the "refill rule." Let them finish their drink before giving them another. Likewise, most of these plants need less water in the winter than during the warmer, brighter summer. When you water, water the whole container and stop when you see water coming out of the drainage holes. This encourages plant roots to grow down into the full volume of soil. This also goes for plants that need very little water, such as succulents. Just dribbling the flat remains from your LaCroix can on the surface is useless.

Light

Many popular houseplants are understory tropicals, meaning they grow low to the ground and are used to the diffused, indirect light that filters down through trees. These species can handle your dank basement or inhumane office setup. Some are tiny green vampires that will sunburn in direct light. One clue that your shade-loving plants *aren't* loving the shade is "leggy" growth: spindly stems stretching as far as possible in search of the sun. Scooch your leggy plants a few feet closer to the window to let them photosynthesize in peace. Other plants, like kitchen herbs and some succulents, need full sun and should get the prime plant real estate of a south-facing window. (Not strong on cardinal directions? It's OK. Your phone has a compass.) If your space is truly troglodytic, inexpensive LED grow bulbs that fit standard lamps are always an option.

Containers

"Containers" is an affected word for pots. Houseplants do best in pots with drainage holes that either sit on top of a saucer or inside a larger pot with no holes (called an indoor container or cachepot). If you want to upcycle plastic containers for your plants, check the little number inside the recycling symbol. Plastics 1, 2, 4, and 5 are nontoxic and food safe. Be sure to add plenty of pencil-width drainage holes with an awl or a drill. Punch the holes from the inside out to prevent water collecting around them inside the pot.

When it comes to containers, *drainage is everything.* If you smell rotten eggs in your home and can rule out a gas leak, a diaper pail, and actual rotten eggs, check your plants. It's a good idea to drain excess water from saucers and cachepots. You can always pour it onto a thirstier plant neighbor. Another tip to avoid general swampiness: Line the inside of your plant pots with used coffee filters. A little coffee is good for plants (caffeine is a natural insecticide), and the water that drains out will be clearer.

Soil

Unless you're highly ambitious or operating at a commercial scale (not recommended for this book's intended audience), bagged, premixed potting soil is ideal. Cacti and succulents do best in light, sandy mixes formulated especially for them. The other plants in this book can handle the generic stuff. Most houseplants bought from a nursery or garden center will be comfortable in their original soil until it's time to repot them.

Repotting

An upgrade to a comfortable and spacious new home is possible . . . for your snake plant. As they grow, most houseplants will eventually need to be repotted to prevent their roots from growing into tight, matted tangles. While it may be tempting to put a small plant in a much bigger pot that it should grow into, most plants find "overpotting" overwhelming and will suffer similarly to plants that get too much water. You wouldn't give your baby hermit crab a *Lord of the Flies*–sized bugle conch to carry around. Don't overpot your plants. If you're short on space to repot plants, you can use the kitchen sink, the bathtub, or a table covered with a tarp made of trash bags and duct tape. When repotting, add fresh soil and fill the container firmly without compacting it. The plant should fit snugly enough to stand on its own. You're buckling your plant baby into a car seat, not a straitjacket. Afterward, give the repotted plant enough water to run through the drainage holes.

Toxicity and Safety

Most houseplants have evolved highly specific defenses to ensure they never end up in your salad. These range from relatively mild (ficus sap that irritates the skin) to catastrophic (aloe latex, a carcinogenic laxative that will turn you inside out). Aroids, the family that includes peace lilies and pothos, contain needle-like calcium oxalate crystals that burn and constrict the throats of mammals who dare to munch. Some houseplants in the asparagus family (e.g., lucky bamboo and spineless yucca) contain saponins, soap-forming compounds that can cause severe nausea and vomiting. I don't care if you're bored, under the influence of a TikTok wellness quack, or have already met the deductible on your health insurance: Apart from basil, cilantro, ginger, and parsley, none of these plants is food. Even the "grow-your-own" trees that come from edible plants, citrus and avocado, are toxic as houseplants. Assess the intelligence and self-control of the creatures in your household and purchase or place your plants accordingly.

The **MOST** pet- and baby-friendly plants in this book are air plants, ginger, heartleaf philodendron, kentia palm, money tree, ponytail palm, and prayer plant.

The **LEAST** pet- and baby-friendly plants are dumb cane, hedgehog cacti, jade plant, pothos, rubber fig, sago palm, and strangling fig.

Bug Basics

Common Houseplant Pests

When you think of plant pests, you might envision a plague of locusts decimating a field of crops. Unfortunately, your houseplants are prone to infestations of their own. These pests are to plant nurseries as cold and flu viruses are to human nurseries: pretty much inevitable. But, with a few tricks up your sleeve, you can keep these bugs at bay. Pest-control guidance for specific plants is included where relevant.

SCALE AND MEALYBUGS

Scale insects are round to oblong in shape, up to $1/4$ inch (6 mm) in length as adults, and range in color from light tan to dark brown. They come in two varieties: soft scale, which is dull and flat, and armored scale, which has a raised, crispy shell. Mealybugs are scale's ickier, fluffier cousins. They're similar in size, but white and hairy. Both bugs have a tough, waxy covering that makes them difficult to kill and control. While you could find these insects anywhere on your plant, you're most likely to see them on the undersides of leaves, hunkered along the midrib. Mealybugs can also hide under the soil surface, and you may see clusters of white, waxy egg masses on affected plants. Both bugs spread easily between plants placed closely together.

Scale insects and mealybugs use their sharp, sucking mouthparts to drink plant sap, which causes leaves to turn yellow and drop. Heavy infestations can slow and stunt plant growth, eventually killing the plant—exsanguination by tiny Tribbles. These bugs produce a sticky fluid called "honeydew" that can appear shiny on plants and is literally a clear warning sign of infestation. If untreated, the honeydew can lead to the development of a dark fungus called "sooty mold" that draws ants. If the ants start seeking out your houseplants instead of your roommate's Dorito crumbs, it's long past time to check for pests.

APHIDS

See a cluster of tiny, pear-shaped insects on your houseplant? If so, it's got aphids, sucking, wingless insects $\frac{1}{8}$ inch (3 mm) or smaller that come in a rainbow of colors. Aphids love tender new shoots and leaves and often cause them to curl under as if they're cringing. Like scale and mealybugs, aphids generate honeydew and can cause leaves to yellow.

SPIDER MITES

Like their fellow pests, spider mites drink sap and cause discoloration and leaf drop. However, these arachnids are so small that you'll see signs of their destruction instead of the bugs themselves: mottled or splotchy foliage, fine webbing, and tiny, shiny eggs on the undersides of leaves. Spider mites love warm, dry environments. When the heat comes on in winter, they bust out like spring breakers in Fort Lauderdale.

Pest Prevention

The best way to prevent an infestation is to start with the healthiest possible plants and then put them in the best possible conditions.

Check plants thoroughly before you buy them.

- What you see is likely the best you will get. Don't assume that a questionable-looking plant for sale is going to look *better* once it's in your hands.

- Inspect the undersides of leaves and the axils, where leaves meet stems. Beware of webbing and yellow, splotchy, or curling foliage.

Regularly inspect your plants once you have them.

- Plants that look healthy in a well-maintained commercial greenhouse may have some ugly surprises in store for you once they encounter your dry, dark home.

Keep new plants and affected plants away from others.

- Monitor new plants for a few weeks before placing them close to others. Resist the plant hoarder/indoor jungle aesthetic if you can. Airflow is beneficial.

Use fresh, sterile potting soil when repotting plants.

- It can be tempting to "recycle" the soil from a dead or afflicted plant or to use soil from open bags that have been sitting outside. Don't. It's not the plant equivalent of wearing the same pair of sweatpants all week; it's more like sharing a beer boot at a frat party where everyone gets mono. Always repot indoor plants into fresh, clean soil.

Follow the plant's care instructions as well as you can.

- A plant that's struggling with the wrong amounts of light and moisture will have a much harder time fighting off pests. Imagine having head lice and a tapeworm while being chronically hungover and eating only Fritos. Attending to basic care goes a long way.

Troubleshooting and Treatment

Still dealing with pests despite your best efforts? Try these escalating interventions:

Prune off the most afflicted leaves or branches.

- The remaining bugs will be easier to target.

Physically remove the insects.

- Depending on the size of the plant and the scale of the infestation (pun intended), you may be able to remove the insects with gloved hands or a wet cloth.

- Give the plant a hard spray of water. This is especially effective for aphids and spider mites. Start with a gentle stream and slowly increase the pressure: You're not pressure-washing your driveway. You don't want to tear away the foliage along with the pests.

- Dip a cotton swab in rubbing alcohol and carefully dab at individual bugs. Be careful not to slather your plant in alcohol: You may need a drink after cleaning up mealybugs, but your plant doesn't.

Discard and start over.

- If you can't salvage the whole plant, try taking cuttings from clean, healthy foliage.

Take the plant on a field trip outside.

- If temperatures are consistently above 50°F (10°C), try putting your affected plant on an open patio or balcony for a few days to a few weeks. Birds love scale and mealybugs. When my big umbrella tree (*Schefflera actinophylla*) was riddled with armored scale, I relished watching the Carolina wrens pick the bugs off like crispy M&M's.

Try a premixed indoor pest spray.

- Ask at your local nursery or garden center about premixed sprays that you can buy in small quantities (available products and formulations may vary by state). These may contain horticultural soaps and oils, which dissolve pests' defensive exteriors and kill them on contact, and/or pyrethrin, a mild pesticide derived from chrysanthemum flowers that breaks down quickly and has low toxicity for humans and pets. You may need to regularly spray affected plants.

- A note on safety: *Always* follow the safety guidelines and instructions on the label. The manufacturers want their products to work for you and have designed their instructions for maximum effectiveness. Any shortcuts or deviations you think of are unlikely to be better. Do you really want to explain to the Poison Control Center that you deliberately misused a pesticide?

- If it's possible to put your plant outside, try that *before* applying any pesticides or products. While these may be safe for indoor use when used as directed, they can be harmful to beneficial insects like bees and butterflies. It's not worth harming local biodiversity just to get the mealybugs off your jade plant.

Get help.

- Done with condescending, unqualified advice on Reddit? Look up your state and county name plus "extension" to find contact information for master gardeners who can help you for free. These enthusiastic experts offer advice tailored to the specific area where you live. Best of all, these folks are not trying to sell you anything.

- Some botanical gardens may have scheduled care clinics where you can bring plants by for a consultation. (*Always* check the event calendar. Don't just march up to the greenhouses with a pest-ridden plant in your arms. There is no houseplant ER.)

Nutrition and Disease Basics

What Is Fertilizer?

Technically, plants eat air: The carbon from carbon dioxide provides most of what plants need to build their structure and mass. But just as humans can't live on orange soda alone, even though it contains water and calories, plants need micronutrients. Most fertilizers provide nitrogen, phosphorous, and potassium, abbreviated as "N-P-K," along with trace minerals. Nitrogen supports foliage growth, phosphorus supports root development and flowering, and potassium is important for stress tolerance. Fertilizer labels indicate the guaranteed percentages of these three nutrients available in the product, such as 20-20-20 or 8-7-6. Plant-specific fertilizers abound, but most houseplants do well with a balanced, all-purpose fertilizer (with roughly equal N-P-K numbers).

Types of Fertilizers

Fertilizers can be synthetic or organic and come in various forms: liquids or liquid concentrates, powders, slow-release granules (the colorful pellets in your potting soil), or spikes. Organic fertilizers are derived from natural materials, such as seaweed, fish emulsion (fluid remains from industrial processing that will make your home smell like a chum bucket; use with discretion), or earthworm castings. Organic fertilizers have a lower concentration of nutrients and deliver them to plants more slowly. Synthetic fertilizers are derived from chemicals and contain higher concentrations of nutrients. Organic fertilizers are to bran muffins as synthetics are to Fun Dip: The latter hits fast, and it's easy to overdo it (in this case, burning or poisoning your plants).

Liquids, liquid concentrates, and powders need to be diluted with water before applying. These are the fastest acting. For forgetful brown thumbs, consider using slow-release granules or fertilizer spikes, which break down slowly over weeks or months. Granules can be mixed into soil when repotting. A safety note about these solid fertilizers: If you use slow-release granules or see them in the soil of plants you've purchased, cover the soil with mulch or keep those plants well out of reach, lest small children or your stoned friends mistake them for Nerds candy. These pellets are the silica gel packets of the plant world: DO NOT EAT.

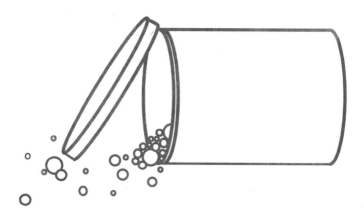

When and How to Fertilize

Plants only need fertilizer while they're actively growing in the spring and summer. In the Northern Hemisphere, fertilize indoor houseplants between March and September, giving them a fall and winter break. Always apply liquid fertilizers to damp soil in order to prevent root damage.

How much fertilizer to use depends on several things. Some plants are enthusiastic feeders (ficus), while others need little fertilizer, if any (most succulents). The larger the container, the brighter the light, and the older the soil, the more fertilizer a plant will need. Newly purchased plants can usually go two to three months without it. Of course, these are not hard-and-fast rules. If you see "concerning colors" or weak stems, give your plant a feed. If your houseplant looks pale or yellow, try fertilizing as often as every two weeks. If your plant then puts forth dark green growth, but with long, leggy stems and smaller leaves than usual, cut back on the fertilizer.

The fertilizer rule of thumb: Don't overdo it. Soluble salts in fertilizers can build up in the soil over time, making it harder for plants to take up water and causing leaf tips to burn. You may also notice a white crust on the soil surface or the inside edges of the pot.

Ultimately, less is more. Just as eating an entire jar of gummy vitamins will not give you superpowers (it *will* give you a brutal headache as you wait to see which end they come back out of), overfertilizing your plants will not make them healthier. Indoor plants need just enough supplementary nutrients for new growth that replaces lost leaves. Overfertilized plants can outgrow their pots or end up scorched and stunted. Always follow product instructions and never use a stronger dosage than indicated on the label. Fertilizer recommendations are included where relevant.

Concerning Colors

Seeing not-green? Try these steps to remedy common ailments.

Gray or white splotches: Powdery mildew

- Prune off affected foliage, then give the plant some space. (It doesn't need time to process emotionally, just increased airflow.)

Black splotches: Sooty mold

- Wear gloves and wipe off this dark slime using a wet paper towel. Barf discreetly. Repeat as needed, but treat any pest issues to keep it from coming back.

Ring spots: Viruses

- Sadly, there is no Tamiflu for houseplants. Discard the specimen to prevent the virus from spreading to other plants.

Yellow leaves with green veins: Houseplant anemia known as "iron chlorosis"

- Lower the soil pH with a sulfur or aluminum sulfate treatment. These are available at garden centers for "acid-

loving plants" (they like a low soil pH, not microdosing LSD). If any of your neighbors are hard-core gardeners, ask around. You may be able to borrow a tablespoon without having to buy an entire pound of the stuff.

- You can also apply a chelated iron spray directly to the plant.

Leaves yellowing from the tips or edges inward: Nitrogen deficiency

- It's hungry! Simply give the plant a dose of fertilizer.

So You Want MORE Plants?*

Tired of buying plants? Have a spouse or partner who's begging you to *stop* buying plants? With some exceptions, most of the plants in this book can be propagated to create more plants. Details are included in the individual profiles. Growing your own plants is satisfying and inexpensive, so you can channel your household budgeting and negotiation efforts into getting more containers for your expanding collection.

Easy Propagation Techniques

Houseplants can be propagated by seed, cuttings, division, and offsets.

SEEDS

The most obvious way to grow a new plant is from seed. Peace lilies, flamingo flowers, umbrella plants, and asparagus ferns can all be grown from seed, but even well-cared-for indoor specimens are unlikely to have what they need to flower and set seeds. Instead, you can buy these seeds online and at some plant nurseries. Be warned: Patience is

 key. These plants may take many months to germinate and much longer to mature. Will staring at a seemingly empty pot for weeks fill you with hope or despair? For a quicker, easier homegrown experience, try sprouting avocado pits or citrus seeds, or sowing basil or cilantro.

Different seeds have different needs. Always check the instructions on the package. While seedling trays are helpful, any clean, shallow, well-draining container will work. All seeds benefit from sterile soil. Look for small bags of seedling mix or seed-starting mix, and moisten the soil before adding the seeds. Most seeds will need to be sown at a specific depth, lightly watered, and then covered and placed in a warm area with a particular amount of light. Once the seeds germinate, don't be alarmed if the first leaves to emerge look nothing like what you're expecting: You probably did read the package correctly. These little imposters are called "seed leaves" and rarely resemble the adult plant. After their "true leaves" emerge, most seedlings are ready for repotting.

CUTTINGS

Succulents like jade plants and vines like philodendron and pothos are easy to grow from cuttings. Using a sharp, clean knife or pair of shears (*not* the giant ones with the orange plastic handles in your kitchen, or the teeny nail scissors languishing in your bathroom drawer), slice off a 4- to 6-inch (10 to 15 cm) segment just below a node (where a leaf meets the stem). Then, trim off the leaves from the bottom half of the cutting. Gently nestle several cuttings 1 to 2 inches (2 to 5 cm) deep in a 6- to 8-inch (15 to 20 cm) diameter plastic pot filled with fresh potting soil. Be sure to use sterile potting soil from a fresh bag. Water the cuttings. Next, put a plastic bag over the top and attach it with a rubber band to make a mini greenhouse. (Please do not start telling people, "I have a greenhouse.") Since the cuttings don't yet have roots to take up water, the high humidity inside the bag will keep them from drying out. Different species need varying amounts of time to take root. Once the roots are about 1 inch (2.5 cm) long, the cuttings can be transferred to their own pots. Look at that. You're a gardening wizard.

DIVISION

Plants like prayer plants, snake plants, ginger, and asparagus ferns grow in big, expanding clusters via tubers or rhizomes (chunky modified roots) underground. You can take these out of their pots, gently break them up into smaller units, repot, and water.

OFFSETS

Aloes, bromeliads, haworthias, hens and chicks, and hedgehog cacti reproduce vegetatively, developing new baby plants (called offsets or "pups") at the base of the parent plant. These can be removed and repotted to grow into new plants. With some species, you may need to wait until the pups reach a certain size or develop roots. Others can be potted up immediately.

Shopping beyond the Garden Center

Displeased with the prices or selection at your local garden center? Unwilling to leave the house? Plants are available online from a variety of sources, from online nurseries and retail behemoths like Amazon to individual growers on Etsy and eBay. Here are some questions to ask before clicking "Add to Cart."

Is the photo accurate and realistic?

- Is there a stock photography watermark?
- Does an image search for the plant species and variety show specimens similar to what's advertised?

What is actually for sale?

- Some growers use sample photos of full-grown plants when selling cuttings or seeds. Always read the product description, lest the SUPER RARE PINK PRINCESS VARIEGATED PHILODENDRON you order on Etsy turns out to be three leaf cuttings in a plastic sandwich bag.

How far will it ship?

- The shorter your plant's trip, the better. Much like myself after a long flight, plants that have traveled far tend to show up desiccated, crotchety, and far from camera-ready. Aim to buy from local or regional sources.

How will it ship?

- Will the plant be shipped potted in soil or bare rooted? Most tropicals will ship in soil, but some larger plant specimens will ship with their bare roots wrapped in burlap or other fabric to reduce shipping weight. If you order a bare-rooted plant, be prepared to pot it up immediately once it arrives. Consider skipping this purchase if the plant will languish in a package locker.

- If you're buying from an individual marketplace seller, do they indicate exactly how they will ship the plant? Professional horticulturists will know what to do; Gary from Tucson, selling his mother-in-law's succulent collection out of spite, might not. No one should go through the trouble of resetting their PayPal password just to be delivered a box of slime.

Any guarantees?

- Experienced, reputable sellers are likely to offer a guarantee. If your plant arrives looking like Big Lots potpourri, do you have any recourse?

Is there any information about how and where the plant was grown?

- Extend the righteous fuss over where your food comes from to where your plants come from and beware of suspiciously cheap plants offered by big retailers. Who knows what conditions they were grown or packed in? Do what you can to support good business practices.

In Defense of Fake Plants

While they don't impact air quality or respond to your presence, artificial plants offer many of the same soothing benefits of real plants. If you still don't trust your two brown thumbs after reading this book and you want a risk-free way to green up your home, get fake plants. You have nothing to prove.

Benefits of Fake Plants

- You can't kill them.

- They last for ages and are extremely low maintenance.

- They're pet- and baby-safe as long as they're made of nontoxic materials and don't have small, loose parts. If a pet does get ahold of a fake plant, the carnage is less disturbing than, say, the trail of faceless, eviscerated plush animals my favorite dogs leave behind.

- They'll look good under any conditions and won't suffer if the light, temperature, or humidity changes. Go ahead and light that weird incense you bought at Bonnaroo!

- You can leave them as long as you want while you're away from home.

How to Select and Display a Good Fake Plant

- The more fake a plant looks in real life, the more convincing the plastic version will be. Fake succulents like donkey tail or hens and chicks tend to look better than fake ficus.

- On fake foliage, look for fraying edges and pixelated patterns that indicate cheap printing. Check for seams and tags that give away plastic stems and branches.

- Give it the "fifty-footer" test. Could it fool *you*?

- Go for foliage over flowers. The less eye-catching, the more convincing.

- Put a fake plant in a real pot, like a ceramic or terra-cotta container.

- Put it in a plausible area. A fake cactus in a dark bathroom isn't fooling anyone, but on a bright windowsill, it just might.

How to Care for Fake Plants

- Dust them. I put my fake succulents in the dishwasher.

- Replace them as needed—for example, if the colors have become bleached by the sun or if the surface develops a waxy, funky coating. Check for numbers on the plastic to see whether you can recycle them.

Difficulty Levels

Practically Plastic

You may forget these low-stakes plants are alive: They won't remind you for weeks or even months. "Practically plastic" plants tolerate neglect (some welcome it) and are ideal for the most forgetful, disorganized, and failure-averse plant owners or for those who travel often. As Dwight Schrute would say, "If [these plants] die, then you've been dead for weeks."

Chill

These are the cats of the houseplant world: They enjoy being left to their own devices, but they still need care. While these plants require more involvement than their "plastic" cousins, they're also more responsive to your efforts. As with cats, you'll want to take pictures and project personalities onto them, but they won't jump onto your shoulders from the top of the refrigerator while you eat cold leftovers straight out of the Tupperware.

Fussy

These plants need regular, though not daily, attention and are ideal for plant owners who remember to floss their teeth and file their taxes. Fussy plants usually have at least one specific need, such as misting with a spray bottle, rotation for even light, regular massages, or a gluten-free diet (just making sure you're still paying attention). A benefit to these higher-maintenance plants is that you can give yourself the credit when they survive!

Master Gardener

Species this demanding are ideal for ambitious, attentive plant owners who want the closest thing to a pet that the plant kingdom can offer. These plants have highly specific needs and/or require daily care to thrive. They're also the most regrettable impulse buys. Beware: These plants may take on an outsized role in your personal life, like *Little Shop of Horrors* without the bloodlust. Only one plant in this book falls under the "master gardener" category: the beloved *Monstera deliciosa*, which millennials continue to buy along with my nemesis, the trendy and capricious fiddle leaf fig (*Ficus lyrata*, not profiled).

Practically Plastic Houseplants

Bird-of-Paradise

(Strelitzia reginae)

Common name: Bird-of-paradise

Botanical name: *Strelitiza reginae*. The genus *Strelitzia* was named after Queen Charlotte Sophia of Mecklenburg-Strelitz (1744–1818), wife of the devastatingly afflicted King George III, a pen pal of Marie Antoinette's, and an amateur botanist who helped expand Britain's Kew Gardens.

Other names: Crane flower

Who it's good for: People who want to be fanned with a giant leaf like ancient royalty; enthusiastic overwaterers; people who like the idea of birds

Appearance: Bird-of-paradise's oblong, gray-green leaves can reach an impressive 4 feet (1.3 m) in length. The leaves emerge on long stems from slightly flattened clusters in the soil. The plant's namesake flowers look like bird heads from the uncanny valley: hard green and orange spathes (beaks) grow at right angles to their stems. Inside, bright orange sepals protect smaller, bright blue petals (crest feathers). When real birds visit these flowers for a sip of nectar, their feet pick up the pollen. Mature, healthy plants can reach 6 feet (2 m) in height and produce up to three dozen flowers per year.

Where you know it from: Large flower arrangements that say "I really mucked up!", overachieving prom corsages, and outlet mall landscaping in southern Florida and California. The bird-of-paradise is also the official flower of the city of Los Angeles.

Where it's actually from: Eastern Cape of South Africa

HOW NOT TO KILL IT

🪴 **Space, pot, and soil requirements:** For a big plant, it doesn't need a deep pot, and a slightly pot-bound bird-of-paradise will produce more flowers. If it's threatening to crack its container, repot it in early spring. Until then, refresh the soil at the top of the pot every year and "feed the birds" (sprinkle in some balanced slow-release fertilizer). Consider using a 2- to 3-inch (5 to 8 cm) layer of mulch around the edge of the soil surface to retain moisture. Just be sure to leave 1 to 2 inches (2 to 5 cm) bare around the stems.

≈ **Water requirements:** Water regularly in spring and summer, allowing the soil to stay somewhat damp. In winter, water only when the soil feels dry. Once a bird-of-paradise is well established, it can tolerate some neglect. If it's too wet or too dry, it'll use the same alarm signal: yellowing leaves. It's up to you to stick your hands in there and assess the cause.

�╬ **Light requirements:** Bird-of-paradise likes a well-lit location but can tolerate partial shade. In the summer, protect this plant from full-on, direct sun.

☠ **Toxicity:** Toxic to dogs and cats (causes nausea and vomiting)

> **Other tips and facts:** It's almost impossible to overfertilize this plant. Bird-of-paradise is a "heavy feeder" that can drink other plants under the table: It's still nipping on nitrogen long after its fellow tropicals have turned to ashes. It's also easy to propagate by division. Just keep your newly divided plants in consistently damp soil. If you want to share or display the flowers, cut bird-of-paradise blossoms last up to two weeks (skip the trip to the florist for that massive apology!). For a unique plastic alternative, LEGO sells a bird-of-paradise model with 1,173 pieces.

Chinese Evergreens

(*Aglaonema spp.*)

Common name:
Chinese evergreens

Botanical names: *Aglaonema commutatum, Aglaonema nitidum,* and *Aglaonema modestum.*

Aglaonema comes from *agalos,* Greek for "bright" or "clear."

Other names: Philippine evergreen, golden evergreen, poison dart plant

Who it's good for: People whose self-care has devolved from "sheet masks" to "sheet cake" and just need a win

Appearance: Chinese evergreens are small, bushy tropical shrubs that max out at around 3 feet (1 m) as houseplants. The leaves often have silvery and pale green splotches. They are easy to confuse with dumb canes (*Dieffenbachia*), their more glamorous South American cousins. An especially attention-grabbing cultivar is the 'Red Edge' (*Aglaonema commutatum* 'Red Edge'), which has electric pink stems and leaf margins.

Where you know it from: The food court at the mall. Who knows how many of these plants have survived being watered with leftover Dr Pepper?

Where it's actually from: Southeast Asia, especially Thailand and the Philippines

HOW NOT TO KILL IT

🪴 **Space, pot, and soil requirements:** Like snake plants, Chinese evergreens are superficial (don't judge them; they can't help it), so wide, shallow pots are ideal. They quickly fill their containers with new little plants, making them easy to propagate by division. Chinese evergreens love high humidity, so get out that spray bottle and mist yours from time to time, especially if it's in a drafty or dry area. These plants don't want to get too cold, either. They'll be cranky at 60°F (15°C) and dead at 45°F (7°C).

≈ **Water requirements:** Light and temperature make a difference for watering this plant. If you can manage it, use room-temperature water that's been sitting out for a while instead of cold water straight from the tap (they're entitled to their preferences, even if they settle for old Dr

Pepper). If your plant is in a particularly dark area, allow the soil to dry out a bit more between waterings. If it's in a brighter space, water once the top 1 inch (2.5 cm) of soil feels dry.

🌾 **Light requirements:** Chinese evergreens thrive under artificial indoor lighting, which makes them ideal for cubicles, basements, even the illegal Airbnb in your crawlspace. If you know where your Chinese evergreen will live, choose its color accordingly: Darker, solid green plants do better in lower light, while silvery, white, and variegated plants can handle brighter light. Just keep them out of direct sunlight. If it's too bright, Chinese evergreens will raise their leaves in defense, a bit like a prayer plant, and their colors may fade.

☠ **Toxicity:** Toxic if eaten (burns the mouth and GI tract)

> **Other tips and facts:** Like their fellow aroids, Chinese evergreens develop tiny flowers that look like baby corncobs in little green hoodies. Pruning these flowers off will help your plant redirect its energy to growing beautiful leaves. It's easier to look pretty when you're not reproducing.

Kentia Palm
(Howea forsteriana)

Common name: Kentia palm

Botanical name: *Howea forsteriana*. The genus is named after Lord Howe Island, Australia. The species is named for Johann Reinhold Forster, a naturalist who accompanied Captain Cook on his second Pacific voyage and was allegedly so insufferable that Cook refused to invite *any* scientists on his third voyage.

Other names: Sentry palm, thatch palm

Who it's good for: Cat owners who want to create jungles for their little tigers and lure them away from the top of the refrigerator

Appearance: The kentia palm has a single trunk that can reach up to 6 feet (2 m) in height as a houseplant and 40 feet (12 m) in the wild. Mature kentia palms look like what a child would draw if told to illustrate a beach. They have a stereotypical crown of dark green, arching leaves, which are divided into narrow segments like big feathers. Though your indoor palm is unlikely to flower, outdoor kentia palms bear giant clusters of starry flowers that develop into small, olive-shaped fruits. The trunks of young palms are green and turn brown over time with sun exposure.

Where you know it from: This is the palm in the lobby of your office building.

Where it's actually from: Lord Howe Island, Australia, a UNESCO World Heritage Site famous for its biodiversity, coral reef, and strict visitor caps

HOW NOT TO KILL IT

⊟ **Space, pot, and soil requirements:** Kentia palms are like New Yorkers in rent-controlled apartments: Why would they ever leave? Drainage is important, but these palms are fine with being root-bound and can stay comfortable in the same container for years. When it's time to repot, be extra careful not to cut or injure the roots. The whole palm will suffer.

≈ **Water requirements:** Follow the refill rule and water thoroughly once the top of the soil feels dry. Kentia palms appreciate some humidity, so if your home is especially dry, mist crispy foliage with a spray bottle. These palms can tolerate some inconsistency when it comes to watering, but don't ignore them like a snake plant or a ZZ plant. They suffer if they dry out completely, and they don't like being overwatered, especially in winter.

🌾 **Light requirements:** Kentia palms aren't picky. They prefer partial to full shade, but can adapt to brighter light and even full sun.

☠ **Toxicity:** Nontoxic

Other tips and facts: Remove old leaves from the bottom of the palm by gently pulling them away. Pruning palms is tricky, and with this one, less is more: Only trim off leaves that are completely dead. Dry palms are susceptible to spider mites, and all palms are at risk of scale. Check your kentia palm regularly for both.

The kentia palm was *the* must-have Victorian houseplant: an 1870s version of my nemesis, the trendy and capricious fiddle-leaf fig (*Ficus lyrata*, not profiled). However, kentia palms are substantially tougher and infinitely more practical. Back on Lord Howe Island, they were used to thatch roofs. The director of the Royal Botanic Garden Sydney visited the island in 1869, and within two years, kentia palms were for sale all over Europe. Demand was somewhere between "1996 Tickle Me Elmo" and "2018 Tesla." The plant's continued popularity is a testament to its sheer indifference to abysmal conditions. You need more fresh air and sunlight than this plant does.

Peace Lilies

(Spathiphylum spp.)

Common name: Peace lilies

Botanical names: *Spathiphyllum* comes from the Greek words for "spathe" and "leaf," referring to the flower. Your peace lily is likely a *Spathiphyllum* x *clevelandii*, a popular hybrid that I consider "the funeral plant." Most mass-produced peace lilies are hybrids of *Spathiphyllum wallisii*, named for German botanist Gustav Wallis. Wallis learned several languages despite being born deaf and introduced more than a thousand plants to Europe (and here I was, impressed with my thirty-day Duolingo streak and two sprouted avocado pits).

Other names: Mauna Loa peace lily, spathe flower, white sails. The name "peace lily" refers to the flower's resemblance to a white flag of surrender. Gift strategically.

Who it's good for: Need to hide an eyesore that a landlord won't fix, like a giant water stain or a defunct radiator? Put a giant 'Sensation' peace lily in front of it.

Appearance: Peace lilies have dark green leaves between 6 and 12 inches (15 and 30 cm) long that narrow at the ends and appear to come straight out of the soil. As on all aroids, the flower is actually that awkward little phallus. The white or colorful "petal" around the outside is a spathe, a modified leaf. Peace lilies bloom year-round. The flowers' white spathes usually turn pale green within two weeks, and the flowers last for several weeks after that.

Peace lilies come in all sizes, from desktop-friendly 'Petite' cultivars to the giant 'Sensation' variety that can reach 6 feet (2 m) in height with a 5-foot (1.5 m) spread, devouring studio apartments. Most peace lilies are between 1 and 3 feet (0.3 and 1 m) tall. If you like freckles, look for the variegated 'Domino' variety.

Where you know it from: The hospital gift shop; Simon Pegg's trusty companion in the 2007 comedy *Hot Fuzz*

Where it's actually from: The tropics of Central America and Southeast Asia

HOW NOT TO KILL IT

🪴 **Space, pot, and soil requirements:** Peace lilies like to be cozy and do well when they're a little bit pot-bound. What can I say? Even the houseplants prefer skinny jeans.

≈ **Water requirements:** Let your peace lily dry out between waterings. If the leaf tips turn brown but the rest of the plant isn't crispy, your peace lily may be unhappy with the chlorine or other chemicals in the water. Leave a container of tap water out overnight, and then water with it the next day (collecting all the half-empty water glasses and seltzer cans from around my house is usually enough for a good soak). Dry, forgotten peace lilies are forgiving and tend to bounce back.

🌥 **Light requirements:** Peace lilies are some of the only easy-care houseplants that bloom in low light. Keep them out of direct sunlight. They like partial shade, and they tolerate heavy shade. However, if it's too dark, they won't flower at all.

☠ **Toxicity:** Toxic if eaten, but safe to handle without gloves

Other tips and facts: Peace lilies do best with light pruning. Trim off brown, wilted flowers and old leaves that have turned yellow. Peace lilies are easy to propagate by division. Just make sure that each new plant has several leaves and don't apply any fertilizer for a few months until new roots have grown in. Plants less than a year old and plants that have recently been divided are less likely to flower. Enjoy their pretty leaves and give them time. No one wants to be pressured to reproduce.

In a NASA study of houseplants' impact on air quality, peace lilies were one of the most effective at removing benzene, carbon monoxide, formaldehyde, and even mold spores. Keep in mind that better air quality is a nice bonus, not a measurable guarantee. No number of houseplants makes it OK to leave wet towels around or ignore the chirp of a dying carbon monoxide detector.

Ponytail Palm

(Beaucarnea recurvata)

Common name: Ponytail palm

Botanical names: *Beaucarnea recurvata* in North America or *Nolina recurvata* in Europe where it spent a gap year it

can't shut up about. *Recurvata* is Latin for "curved backward."

Other names: Bottle palm, elephant foot tree, ponytail plant. This plant is mistakenly referred to as a palm because most specimens have a single trunk with all leaves emerging from the top. By that logic, a possum is a "kitty cat" just because it walks on all fours and tried to get on top of the refrigerator when it came in the house.

Who it's good for: Space cadets, couch potatoes, and combinations thereof: space potatoes. The ponytail palm was described by former botanical garden director Gerald Klingaman as "a godsend for the disorganized, seeming to thrive on mistreatment that would kill most houseplants." These plants are also ideal for dry climates. If you're running dehumidifiers, this is your plant. (The only other creatures as excited about a dehumidifier are the spider mites lying in wait on your tropical houseplants.)

Appearance: The ponytail palm has a distinctive, bottom-heavy trunk called a caudex that stores water and usually tapers to a single stem. Older plants may have multiple branches. The leaves emerge in a spray of curly ribbons like a Hallmark movie actress's criminally overprocessed hair. Wild and outdoor specimens can reach a height of 30 feet (10 m) and a diameter of 7 feet (2.3 m). Houseplants tend to max out at 6 to 8 feet (2 to 2.5 m) with a 3- to 5-foot (1 to 1.5 m) spread. Houseplants rarely bloom, but mature outdoor plants can produce large clusters of small, white flowers.

Where you know it from: I once saw a drunk man at a party turn to a ponytail palm at eye level and ask it, "So, what do you do?" The elephant habitat at the San Diego Zoo is also landscaped with mature *Beaucarnea*, which I worry sets up unrealistic beauty standards for the elephants.

Where it's actually from: Semidesert areas of Belize, Guatemala, and southeastern Mexico

HOW NOT TO KILL IT

⊟ **Space, pot, and soil requirements:** The ponytail palm likes a relatively small pot and a sandy soil mix that encourages drainage. Smaller pots encourage slower growth. Take advantage of this. Big specimens can become heavy and unwieldy and are not worth slipping a disc over. These are some of the happiest houseplants in winter, because they enjoy the dry, heated indoor air that torches unmisted tropicals.

≈ **Water requirements:** Follow the refill rule with this plant: Water deeply, then let it dry completely between waterings. Reduce watering even further during the winter. If the leaf tips turn brown, the plant may be unhappy with the fluoride in your water. It's not a conspiracy theorist; it just metabolizes minerals differently.

Please don't overwater this plant. I once had the misfortune of helping to excise a 30-year-old, 20-foot-tall ponytail palm that died of root rot due to lack of drainage. The dead tissue collapsed into a putrid mucus that had to be shoveled out, bucket by bucket. It left a 10-foot crater and still gives me nightmares. Err on the side of dryness.

🔥 **Light requirements:** The ponytail palm loves full sun but can tolerate up to six months of shade.

☠ **Toxicity:** Nontoxic

> **Other tips and facts:** Old leaves will turn yellow and dry out on healthy plants. Simply prune or peel them off.

Pothos

(Epipremnum aureum)

Common name: Pothos

Botanical name: *Epipremnum aureum*, from the Greek, meaning "gold upon a tree trunk"

Other names: Golden pothos, money plant, ivy arum, devil's ivy, devil's vine

Who it's good for: People who are disappointed to have finished growing out their bangs; roommates in favor of the beaded curtain who were outvoted

Appearance: Pothos has trailing, climbing vines that can grow up to 40 feet (12 m) with glossy, heart-shaped leaves. Golden pothos is streaked or speckled with yellow. The 'Neon' variety is pure acid green, while the 'Marble Queen' has swirls of dark green and white.

Where you know it from: The dusty basket on top of your mom's white kitchen cabinets, circa 1995

Where it's actually from: The Solomon Islands, east of Papua New Guinea in the South Pacific

HOW NOT TO KILL IT

🝳 **Space, pot, and soil requirements:** Pothos likes to hang out. It does best in a basket or on a shelf, table, or other piece of furniture where its long vines can trail downward. With a trellis or a textured post, it can also climb upward. Either way, give it (vertical) space.

≈ **Water requirements:** Pothos follows the refill rule. Overwatering can cause leaf tips and edges to turn black. Drain excess water from saucers or cachepots.

🌿 **Light requirements:** This plant likes bright, indirect light and can tolerate some shade. It can be happy in almost any room that is well lit or has windows.

☠ **Toxicity:** Highly toxic if eaten

Other tips and facts: Don't be afraid to prune your pothos if the vines become too long. Pothos pruned to within 2 to 3 inches (5 to 7.5 cm) of the soil surface will grow back stronger than ever. (If only a good haircut did so much for us.) Pruning pothos is also a great opportunity to try propagation with cuttings. Trim off a segment with at least four leaves, right above a node. Place the cut end in a glass of clean water and leave it indirect light for a few weeks until new roots form. If the water looks murky, replace it.

There's a reason you recognize this glossy vine from miserable public spaces: It will grow anywhere. If this plant manages to die, please look into major public health threats in your area.

For this reason, robust pothos needs to stay in the pot. If you have a yard and live in a warm area, resist any temptation to plant it outside. In the wild, thick, mature vines can produce light-scavenging leaves more than 2 feet (60 cm) long. Let's not replace kudzu with a prettier, but worse, invasive species.

With its colorful, dangling vines, pothos can be especially tempting for cats and small children. For an alternative that will keep you in the ASPCA's good graces, try heartleaf philodendron.

Snake Plants

(Dracaena trifasciata and Dracaena angolensis)

Common name: Snake plants

Botanical names: Mother-in-law's tongue is *Dracaena trifasciata*, also known as *Sansevieria trifasciata*.

Viper's bowstring is known as *Dracaena angloensis* and *Sansevieria cylindrica*. I own both plants and bought them for their names alone.

Other names: African spear, bowstring hemp

Who it's good for: The most anxious or least ambitious of plant owners. You couldn't kill this plant with a chainsaw (the pieces would take root). You'd need a woodchipper.

Appearance: Snake plants have no stems or branches. Their thick, leathery leaves emerge straight from the soil out of a thick rhizome (a fleshy, root-like stem). Mother-in-law's tongue has flat dark green leaves with wavy, gray stripes, and the popular 'Laurentii' variety has a bright yellow edge. They can reach 4 feet (1.3 m) but tend to max out at 2 feet (60 cm). Viper's bowstring has pointy, tubular leaves about 1 inch (2.5 cm) wide and can reach up to 6 feet (2 m). You may see viper's bowstring sold in a braided form, like lucky bamboo on anabolic steroids.

Where you know it from: Every manner of unpleasant waiting room: the dentist's office, the gastroenterologist's office, the marriage and family therapist's office . . .

Where it's actually from: Tropical western Africa. Mother-in-law's tongue is from Nigeria and viper's bowstring is from Angola.

HOW NOT TO KILL IT

🪴 **Space, pot, and soil requirements:** As tough as these plants are, they're very shallow. (It's a survival strategy, really, not to engage with deeper levels of their experience.) Use a wide, shallow, heavy pot to prevent your snake plant from toppling over and fill it with a sandy potting mix that drains well. If you're willing to clean up the shards, you can wait to repot a snake plant until it cracks its current pot. The plant will be fine. Snake plants can handle your HVAC, too: They tolerate dry air and are comfortable down to 50°F (10°C).

≈ **Water requirements:** The snakes are not thirsty. Overwatering is a no-no. While you couldn't kill this plant with a chainsaw, you absolutely *can* kill it with root rot. Follow the refill rule and let the soil dry out completely between waterings. In winter, snake plants only need water once every one to two months. Water from the edges, not directly over the center of the plant. Snake plants tolerate drought and will be very forgiving if you overlook them. In today's attention economy, their indifference is downright refreshing.

☀ **Light requirements:** Snake plants prefer a warm spot with bright light. They can tolerate shade, but their leaves won't grow as thick or tall as they could. Keep them out of direct, hot midday sun.

☠ **Toxicity:** Mildly toxic if eaten (saponins)

Other tips and facts: Snake plants are easy to propagate by division when repotting. (Isn't that what everyone wants, a family of snakes?) Only fertilize your snake plant if it's in a bright, hot area. Once or twice per summer is plenty.

Mother-in-law's tongue first became popular in the United States in the 1920s and '30s because it was sold in Woolworth department stores. In the 1970s, NASA-funded research found that mother-in-law's tongue improves air quality by removing pollutants like ammonia, formaldehyde, and benzene. Other research since then has shown that snake plants can absorb tobacco smoke and fumes from carpet and paint. One plant per 100 square feet (9 square m) is enough to make a difference. However, no number of houseplants can compensate for roommates who rip bongs in clear violation of a lease agreement and/or state laws. More herbs are not the answer to *that* problem.

Snake plants are in the asparagus family (DO NOT EAT) and their leaves contain long, parallel fibers. Snake plant fibers were historically used to make bowstrings, but I don't recommend you do anything with yours other than use it to fill that awkward corner in your living room.

Spineless Yucca

(Yucca elephantipes)

Common name: Spineless yucca

Botanical names: *Yucca elephantipes*, also known as *Yucca guatemalensis* and *Yucca gigantea*. The name "yucca" comes from the word for cassava (a similar but unrelated plant) in Carib, a language indigenous to northeastern South America (not to be confused with *carob*, the 1970s chocolate alternative that tastes like dust and terrorized a generation of dieters).

Other name: Soft-tip yucca

Who it's good for: Ikea impulse shoppers who arrived too late in the day to get a money plant; fans of Joshua Tree National Park who understand that you can't just, like, dig up a souvenir

Appearance: "Spineless" yucca isn't cowardly; it lacks the barbs that make its relatives too dangerous to keep indoors (Joshua Tree and Spanish bayonet). These plants have spiraling rosettes of thin, blue-green, sword-shaped leaves that grow up to 4 feet (1.3 m) long and 3 inches (7.5 cm) wide. The trunk widens at the base with age (don't we all?) and develops a rough, cracked texture that looks like an elephant's foot. In the wild, these plants can reach 30 feet (10 m) in height. Indoor houseplants are much smaller and rarely flower.

Where you know it from: Folks going hard for a Southwestern vibe—cow skull and striped ponchos on the wall, burning sage, dabbling in peyote—even though they're from freaking Minneapolis

Where it's actually from: Mexico and Guatemala

HOW NOT TO KILL IT

🪴 **Space, pot, and soil requirements:** Yucca likes sandy soil, so a succulent or cactus mix works great. Drainage is imperative. To keep your plant at a manageable size, use a small, cozy container and repot infrequently.

≈ **Water requirements:** Follow the refill rule and allow the soil to dry out between waterings. In the winter, scale back and give your plant just enough water to prevent its uncharacteristically dramatic leaf drop. Spineless yucca tolerates drought, but not overwatering. Damp soils will lead to root rot.

☈ **Light requirements:** Spineless yucca isn't picky about light. It loves full sun but can settle for partial shade.

☠ **Toxicity:** Toxic if eaten (saponins)

Other tips and facts: Unless the size is getting out of control, spineless yucca needs little to no pruning. Like dragon tree and corn plant, this plant will send forth new growth just below a cut stem and can be propagated by cuttings. Offshoots from the base of the plant take root easily.

Historically, yucca plants have been used to make a wide variety of products. Leaf fibers can be woven into ropes, baskets, and textiles. Some species' blossoms are edible and high in potassium and calcium, and some roots can be used to make soap. However, your spineless yucca is just a quiet, herbaceous friend. Please do not eat any part of it.

ZZ Plant

(*Zamioculcas zamiifolia*)

Common name: ZZ plant

Botanical name: *Zamioculcas zamiifolia*. Both names reflect the plant's resemblance to

zamias, cycads from the tropical Americas, but this fleshy baby is all aroid (related to peace lilies and elephant ears).

Other names: Cardboard palm, Zuzu plant, Zanzibar gem, eternity plant. Other common names include the aroid palm and eternity palm, which are even more of a stretch than "ponytail palm" or "sago palm." This plant doesn't even have a trunk.

Who it's good for: Plant owners living in the bleakest of conditions. Even if the walls of your apartment are windowless cinderblocks and a bedsheet tacked to the ceiling, you can still have a beautiful ZZ plant.

Appearance: ZZ plants' tapered, rubbery round stems emerge straight from the soil and have dark, glossy, elliptical leaves alternating along one side. Fully grown plants can reach 3 feet (1 m). If repotted consistently, they can reach a maximum spread of 5 feet (1.5 m). You may find flowers at the base of stems (those tiny, shrouded phalluses).

Where you know it from: It's the one in the office that looks like plastic, but isn't, and it's the only plant that can survive six months of your coworkers making the same mistake.

Where it's actually from: The dry grasslands of eastern Africa

HOW NOT TO KILL IT

🖫 **Space, pot, and soil requirements:** Most ZZ specimens are sold in pots that are a bit too small, but the plant will still do well for a long time in its original container. When it does get too big for its breeches, repot it in a regular potting mix and add some pebbles or gravel at the bottom for drainage.

≈ **Water requirements:** Do not water this plant. Well, water it every two to three weeks if you absolutely must. Less is more. Always let this plant dry out between waterings. This tardigrade among houseplants can survive without water for three to four months. If the leaves or stems start turning yellow, you've overdone it.

🌿 **Light requirements:** The ZZ plant likes partial shade but will tolerate anything short of complete darkness. If kept in too dark a room, the plant will get leggy and send out longer, thinner branches to search for light. There are no reports of it reaching and flipping a switch . . . yet.

☠ **Toxicity:** Toxic if eaten. Sap is irritating. Wear rubber gloves to prune and repot.

> **Other tips and facts:** ZZ plants make great housewarming gifts. Happy in most environments, these plants make their recipients feel like capable adults and will live long enough to be subtle reminders of your generosity for years.
>
> This plant's ability to thrive with as little care as possible flies in the face of logic and is both thrilling and terrifying. It only needs fertilizer once or twice a year, and it doesn't get brown leaf tips from hard water. Pruning off flowers encourages heartier foliage growth.
>
> Want a goth version? Look for the Dowon (Raven™ ZZ) cultivar.

Chill Houseplants

Aloe
(Aloe vera)

Common name: Aloe

Botanical names: *Aloe vera*, formerly known as *Aloe* *barbadensis*. The name aloe means "bitter" and comes from the Arabic *alloch* or the Greek *allal*.

Other names: Medicinal aloe, true aloe

Who it's good for: Kitchen klutzes prone to minor burns; people who want a classic succulent that's easy to replace if a roommate goes on a misguided wellness bender and overharvests it

Appearance: Aloe plants grow in stemless rosettes of lance-shaped, succulent leaves up to 18 inches (45 cm) long. The leaves have pale white spots and pointy "teeth" along the margins. Mature plants can reach up to 3 feet (1 m) tall. In ideal conditions with plenty of sunlight, they may flower in summer, sending up clusters of yellow blossoms at the ends of long stalks.

Where you know it from: It was in that chunky soft drink from the farmers' market that led to the unspeakable gas incident. It's also the highest-touch surface in any public succulent collection, usually broken and oozing. Aloes are popular as landscape plants in dry, frost-free areas such as Southern California, where hummingbirds fight turf wars over their flowers.

Where it's actually from: Aloes are native to the southern Arabian Peninsula, southeast Africa, and Madagascar. The *Aloe vera* we know and love doesn't exist in nature (it's been shaped by years of breeding, like a French bulldog among wolves), but the most similar natural plants can be found in Oman.

HOW NOT TO KILL IT

🪴 **Space, pot, and soil requirements:** Aloes love sandy soil mixes that hold very little water. Since aloe plants grow asymmetrically and can become very top-heavy, use heavy clay or ceramic pots to prevent them from tipping over. Unless your plant is busting out of its container, it can handle being bit pot-bound. To keep your aloe small, repot infrequently. To encourage your aloe to grow larger, repot it annually. Aloes like dry climates, but keep yours away from vents or drafty windows.

≈ **Water requirements:** Water your aloe when the top 1 inch (2.5 cm) of soil is dry and follow the refill rule. If water collects in a cachepot or saucer, pour it out. Never let your aloe sit in standing water: There's a fine line between healthy gel and dying goo. Unlike some kalanchoes, which develop a pink edge or sheen in optimal conditions, pale red aloe leaves are a sign of dryness and poor soil. If your aloe's leaves start to look like winter strawberries, grab the watering can.

🔆 **Light requirements:** Aloes love full sun and need it in order to flower, but they tolerate bright, indirect light. If your aloe lives by a window, rotate the plant occasionally so that all sides get sufficient light. If you move an aloe plant from the shade into full sun too quickly, it may sunburn (ironic, given the plant's uses).

☠ **Toxicity:** Toxic to pets if eaten. Topical use of gel is safe for humans.

Other tips and facts: You can easily propagate aloe from the pups that grow at the base of a mature plant. Once the pups have roots, they can be removed and repotted.

Medicinal and healing uses of aloe predate Christianity, and aloe can be found in cosmetic and wellness products all over the world. The safest and most common way to use aloe is to apply the gel topically as a moisturizer or to relieve minor burns. Simply break off a leaf and apply directly to the affected area. If you don't plan to use your aloe plant as a remedy, consider buying a decorative, colorful variety such as 'Bright Star' or 'Pink Blush'.

What about eating it? While it's possible that aloe gel can be used safely as a food, completely separating it from the rest of the leaf is imperative. The outer skin of the leaf and the yellow latex between the skin and the gel are carcinogenic and dangerous. The latex is considered a drug by the FDA: It's a ruthless laxative that can cause kidney damage and even death if taken in high doses. Consuming aloe as a food can also interfere with medications. Please don't start putting whole aloe leaves into your smoothies. How will you recommend this book to your friends if you're dead?

Asparagus Ferns

(Asparagus setaceus and Asparagus densiflorus)

Common name: Asparagus ferns

Botanical names: *Asparagus setaceus* and *Asparagus densiflorus*. The genus name *Asparagus* is no coincidence: These plants are related to the asparagus we buy bundled with purple rubber bands (DO NOT EAT). They're not actually ferns. *Densiflorus* refers to the flowers that cluster densely within the foliage and *setaceus* means "bristly." (Feeling a little setaceus today?)

Other names: *A. densiflorus* is also known as Sprenger's asparagus fern. The 'Myersii' variety is often sold as foxtail asparagus.

Who it's good for: People who would like to stroke a houseplant the way a Bond villain strokes a cat. *A. densiflorus* has an especially tactile, Koosh-ball quality.

Appearance: Though most houseplants appear shrubby and compact, asparagus ferns are evergreen, bushy vines with climbing stems that grow tough and spiny with age (don't we all?) and can reach up to 20 feet (6 m) in the wild. *A. setaceus* has flat, fern-like foliage, while *A. densiflorus* has fluffy, cone-shaped branches. Asparagus ferns may put forth tiny white flowers in late spring that develop into toxic red berries. Both species have small thorns.

The popular 'Myersii' variety, or foxtail asparagus, has pointy, upright stems and tends to max out at a convenient 2-foot (60 cm) height and 4-foot (1.3 m) spread. Another reason to look for this variety is that it produces fewer berries and is less of an invasive threat if kept outside. It's believed that this plant is named for Frank Nicholas Meyer, an agricultural explorer for the USDA (a real job in the early 1900s!) who brought over 2,500 plant species to the United States from Asia, including Meyer lemons.

Where you know it from: Read labels carefully at the garden center: This one looks like dill. You may have also seen asparagus ferns along roadsides and in woodlands where they've escaped cultivation. These fluffy fugitives are considered invasive weeds in Hawai'i, Texas, and Florida.

Where it's actually from: Southern and eastern Africa

HOW NOT TO KILL IT

🗑 **Space, pot, and soil requirements:** These plants prefer a dark, rich soil that's well drained, but will tolerate just about anything (like how I love sea bass but will put away a box of fish sticks without hesitation). Asparagus ferns may need to be repotted every year in early spring. They can easily outgrow their containers, and the dense roots are strong enough to break pots. Thick ceramic containers are ideal.

≋ **Water requirements:** Water asparagus ferns regularly to keep their soil consistently damp. Back off a bit in the winter, but don't let them dry out completely. Once well established, asparagus ferns can tolerate some watering neglect. They do not need high humidity and may do better in dry homes that would leave real ferns in a crunchy pile on the floor.

🔆 **Light requirements:** Asparagus ferns like indirect light to partial shade. Hot, direct sun can cause the foliage to turn yellow. In full shade, the foliage may turn pale green. Turn up the light for maximum ferret-like foliage: Asparagus ferns in brighter light tend to be denser and more compact than those grown in darker conditions.

☠Toxicity: The berries are toxic if eaten (they cause vomiting and diarrhea in pets). The sap causes contact dermatitis (itchy, swollen skin). Handle with gloves.

> **Other tips and facts:** To prune your asparagus fern, trim stems and branches to maintain the plant's size and shape and to encourage denser growth. Cut old, yellowed stems off at the base. Any stems cut back to the soil level will regenerate. Asparagus ferns can be propagated by division.
>
> Don't be alarmed if your plant drops some leaves in winter. It's normal.

Basil

(Ocimum basilicum)

Common name: Sweet basil

Botanical name: *Ocimum basilicum*. *Ocimum* comes from the Greek okimon, meaning "aromatic herb."

Other names: Great basil, Genovese basil. There are dozens of basil varieties and hybrids, such as Thai basil (*O. basilicum* var. *thyrsiflora*) that are fun to grow at home. These guidelines are for the "grocery store basil" that's easiest to come by in the United States.

Who it's good for: People tired of the salty mush that passes for pesto in North American supermarkets; people tired of spending five dollars on fresh herbs that turn to sludge in the refrigerator

Appearance: Basil plants are soft, shrubby herbs that average 12 to 18 inches (30 to 45 cm) in height. Depending on the variety, the ovate leaves can be anywhere from 1/2 inch (1 cm) (Greek basil) to 6 inches (15 cm) long (Italian large leaf). Colors range from electric green to moody dark purple.

Where you know it from: Many a caprese salad

Where it's actually from: Tropical Africa to tropical Asia

HOW NOT TO KILL IT

⊟ **Space, pot, and soil requirements:** Basil thrives in terra-cotta pots, but will settle for plastic. Go for the richest, darkest organic potting soil you can get.

≈ **Water requirements:** Keep it moist, but don't drown it. If your plant is close to the kitchen sink, there's no excuse.

⚶ **Light requirements:** Like most Italophiles, basil prefers the full sun.

☠ **Toxicity:** Nontoxic

Other tips and facts: Keep it warm! Cold temperatures stunt growth, and if the air or soil reaches 50°F (10°C) or lower, the leaves will turn black. Bring your basil plants in from the window during the winter and never put basil in the fridge.

Pinching off any long stems and flower buds will encourage your basil plant to grow more flavorful leaves. Only harvest a few leaves at a time while your plant is small. Once it's fully grown, you can pinch off entire stems or tips. Place the stems in a cup of water if you're not using them immediately.

Unlike most plants in this book, Italian basil species are annual, meaning they will eventually die in your care. Don't blame yourself! Some Thai and African basil varieties are perennial and can last a few years. Check before buying. Fortunately, basil is one of the easiest herbs to grow from seed. Place a few basil seeds in a small pot of soil. Keep it moist and in full sun, and within a month, you'll be making pesto. Repeat this every week or two for a continual supply. *Prego!*

Cilantro and Parsley

(Coriandrum sativum and Petroselinum crispum)

Common names:
Cilantro and parsley

Botanical names: *Coriandrum sativum* and *Petroselinum crispum*. *Coriandrum* comes from the Greek *koris*, which refers to the unripe fruits' unpleasant odor. This mercifully disappears once the ripe fruits have dried out (your plants may not live long enough to flower and set seed, eliminating the problem altogether). Parsley's genus name comes from *petros*, Greek for "rock," and selinon, which refers to parsley or celery. *Crispum* means "wavy" or "curled."

Other names: Cilantro is also known as coriander. The dry seeds are a popular spice used in curry powders and garam masala.

Who it's good for: "Foodies" who correct everyone's pronunciation of "pho" but always order the fried rice when no one else is watching

Appearance: Cilantro is a soft annual (replanted every year) that grows in clumps up to 2 feet (60 cm) tall and 18 inches (45 cm) across. Young plants have wide, flat, lacy leaves that are used as a fresh herb. Cilantro's pink or white flowers grow in showerhead-shaped clusters called umbels. The seeds develop in tiny, rounded pods that turn yellow and darken as they ripen.

Parsley is a biennial herb. It grows into a plant, overwinters, then sets seed and dies the following year. Parsley grows in clumps up to 12 inches (30 cm) tall and wide. Its triangular, dark green leaves are divided into flat and fine (Italian variety) or tight and curly leaflets (Hamburg variety). When parsley flowers in its second year, it grows tall stalks with umbels of greenish-yellow flowers.

Where you know it from: Cilantro is the divisive herb sprinkled across your pad Thai, pho, and fish tacos. Some people think cilantro tastes like soap, either due to aldehyde compounds in the plant or to having no taste to begin with. Italian parsley gives tabbouleh its fresh, zesty flavor. Hamburg parsley is the dark, curly thing next to the slice of lemon on your plate of fish.

Where it's actually from: Cilantro is native to southern Europe and the western Mediterranean region. Parsley is native to Greece and the Balkans.

HOW NOT TO KILL IT

⊟ **Space, pot, and soil requirements:** You can grow cilantro and parsley together in any food-safe container (ceramic; terra-cotta; plastics 1, 2, 4, or 5) with good drainage. If planting it yourself, use a fresh bag of organic potting soil. Cilantro and parsley grow well in cool, dry indoor conditions.

≈ **Water requirements:** Cilantro and parsley like regular, deep watering that keeps their soil moderately damp. Do not allow these herbs' soil to dry out (that's not how herbs are dried for later use).

≋ **Light requirements:** These herbs like bright light but tolerate partial shade. A kitchen window is a great spot as long as they don't broil in direct afternoon sun.

⚘ **Toxicity:** Cilantro is nontoxic to pets, but parsley is toxic to pets. Basil is a pet-safe alternative to parsley.

Other tips and facts: Harvest these herbs from the outside in instead of from the top down. Trim off flower stalks to encourage flavorful foliage.

Cilantro and parsley are *old* herbs. Cilantro has been cultivated in India and China for thousands of years and was even grown in ancient Egypt. Spanish conquistadors introduced cilantro to Peru and Mexico (not a fair trade). Historical medicinal uses included immortality potions (well, it worked for cilantro cultivation, if not for the eaters), appetite stimulants, aphrodisiacs, sedatives, and digestive aids. Please only use yours as an herb and add it to food right before serving.

Parsley has been popular in Europe since the Middle Ages. An old superstition alleged that only witches or pregnant women could grow parsley, but this herb is benignly indifferent to its growers' fertility or mastery of magic.

Dumb Canes

(Dieffenbachia spp.)

Common name: Dumb canes. "Dumb" refers to the consequences of eating this plant: paralyzed vocal cords that leave the eater speechless.

Botanical names: *Dieffenbachia seguine, Dieffenbachia amoena.* The genus is named for J. F. Dieffenbach, who managed the gardens of Schönbrunn Palace in Vienna in the 1830s. He is not to be confused with the *other* J. F.

the *other* J. F. Dieffenbach, the Napoleonic war veteran and surgeon who invented hair plugs in Berlin around the same time.

Other names: Exotica perfection (also my stripper name, according to a BuzzFeed quiz), leopard lily, tropic snow (also 1980s slang for cocaine, which I learned the hard way from a very awkward transaction at a now-closed garden center in South Atlanta)

Who it's good for: If you enjoy the irony of a "camo print" houseplant, get a dumb cane.

Appearance: Dumb canes have brilliantly patterned, oblong, pointed leaves that can reach about 1 foot (30 cm) in length. The "cane" is a segmented stem that resembles bamboo and can reach 1 to 2 inches (2.5 to 5 cm) in thickness. Like Chinese evergreens and ZZ plants, dumb canes can grow little aroid flowers, but they're rare. Dozens of cultivars are available in a wide range of colors and patterns, from nearly pure white to speckled with green and yellow splotches of every size.

Where you know it from: This is a popular one that you've likely seen in garden centers and on shaded patios. I know it from my frog terrarium, where its rapid growth threatens to lift the lid enough for my slime babies to escape.

Where it's actually from: The Caribbean and tropical South America

HOW NOT TO KILL IT

🏺 **Space, pot, and soil requirements:** Dumb canes do best if regularly repotted (any potting soil and well-drained container will do), but it's not urgent. You can get away with heavy pruning that would destroy most other plants.

≈ **Water requirements:** Follow the refill rule. As long as the top 1 inch (2.5 cm) of the soil is dry, it's OK to go ahead and water. Ease up during the winter. Dumb canes like it humid, so give yours an occasional mist from a spray bottle.

🔆 **Light requirements:** Dumb canes can handle almost all light conditions, except for full, direct sun. Dumb canes slant toward the light, so rotate your plant regularly for even growth.

☠ **Toxicity:** Toxic if eaten. The sap is highly irritating to skin. Wear gloves when pruning and repotting.

Other tips and facts: These plants grow quickly. If your dumb cane gets too big, simply hack it back to your desired height (6 inches/15 cm minimum) and it will put forth new leaves right below the cut. Always wear gloves to handle this plant and don't touch your mouth or eyes before washing your hands, unless you've always wondered what pepper spray feels like.

Like the most regrettable people you've ever dated, dumb canes are beautiful, but toxic. If any creatures in your household are prone to foraging, prayer plants are a safe alternative.

Flamingo Flowers

(Anthurium andraeanum and Anthurium scherzerianum)

Common names: Flamingo flowers, tail flowers

Botanical names: *Anthurium andraeanum* and *Anthurium scherzerianum*. The genus name comes from *anthos*, Greek for

"flower," and *oura*, meaning "tail." If the Greeks themselves had named this plant, they might've referred to a different body part.

Other names: Flamingo flower is also known as painter's

palette, and tail flower is also known as pigtail plant.

Who it's good for: Fans of The Lonely Island's "Dick in a Box" *Saturday Night Live* sketch; people who want bright flowers that last for six weeks with little care

Appearance: These plants are epiphytes, meaning they grow on top of trees and other plants in the wild. They have dark green, heart-shaped leaves up to 8 inches (20 cm) long that point downward. The leaf stems emerge straight from the base of the plant. As houseplants, they grow to about 16 inches (40 cm) tall. The flower is the "tail," the pale-yellow spadix (gherkin-esque appendage) surrounded by a large, waxy spathe, a modified leaf that looks like a giant petal. Flowers last for several weeks, and healthy plants should bloom year-round.

Where you know it from: Seasonal grocery store displays around Valentine's Day. Is it a heart? Is it a phallus? Let the recipient decide.

Where it's actually from: Columbia, Ecuador, and Costa Rica

HOW NOT TO KILL IT

🖮 **Space, pot, and soil requirements:** Plastic pots like the ones these plants are sold in are completely fine. Adding mulch helps retain soil moisture and hide roots and fertilizer granules at the soil surface. These anthuriums do best if repotted every two years (if you can keep yours alive that long). If you do repot one, don't put it in stodgy, thick soil: These plants grow on trees in the wild, so they like all the drainage they can get.

≈ **Water requirements:** No refill rule for these plants, and no winter break: Keep the soil moist (not soaked) year-round, and do not let it dry out. These plants also like humidity, so give them a mist. If the humidity drops below 50 percent, they'll start to lose their shiny texture, and the leaves may scorch. Keep them away from drafty areas.

☀ **Light requirements:** Give these plants bright, indirect light, but not full sun. If it's too dark, they may not bloom. They'll be happiest near a south- or west-facing window.

☠ **Toxicity:** Toxic if eaten but safe to handle without gloves

Other tips and facts: These plants are a great option for people who want to give flowers as gifts, but not bouquets that will wilt and draw fruit flies within days (unless you *want* your gift to be petty and backhanded, in which case, go for the fruit flies). Plants of both species will produce about four to six flowers a year. If you cut the flowers, they will last for several weeks in a vase of water. Trim off dying flowers to encourage new growth. Propagate by division when repotting.

You may need to dust your anthuriums with a damp cloth. The waxier a plant looks, the more noticeable the dust will be.

Flapjacks and Paddle Plants

(Kalanchoe spp.)

Common names: Flapjacks, paddle plant, panda plant, kalanchoe. Many pronunciations abound, but the correct one is "kal-un-KOH-ee."

Botanical names: Commonly available houseplants include *Kalanchoe blossfeldiana* (florist kalanchoe), *Kalanchoe pinnata* (air plant kalanchoe), *Kalanchoe daigremontiana* (mother-of-thousands), *Kalanchoe luciae* (flapjacks), and *Kalanchoe tomentosa* 'Panda' (panda plant).

Other names: Desert cabbage, dog's tongue, chandelier plant, devil's backbone

Who it's good for: People who like succulents, but don't think cacti or aloes look freaky enough. Florist kalanchoe is good for people who want flowering indoor plants for the winter but think poinsettias are overdone and holiday cacti are "for boomers."

Appearance: The most common species, florist kalanchoe (*K. blossfeldiana*), has thick, glossy leaves with a serrated edge and delicate, four-petaled flowers in warm colors that last for several months in the winter. Flapjacks (*K. luciae*) and panda plant (*K. tomentosa* 'Panda') are grown for their foliage. Flapjacks' rounded, red-edged leaves stack horizontally like pancakes. Panda plant's plump, oval-shaped leaves have a soft, silver fuzz and a serrated edge tipped in brown that makes them look like bear paws. The air plant kalanchoe (*K. pinnata*) and mother-of-thousands (*K. daigremontiana*) produce tiny new plantlets along the leaf edges that drop off and take root close to the parent plant.

Where you know it from: Mother-of-thousands was inconveniently on the cover of both your high school geometry *and* biology textbooks. Florist kalanchoe is popular in gift shops and its leaves look like someone got carried away with the pinking shears. If you've seen a succulent that looked like a bunch of weird tongues, it was probably a flapjacks.

Where it's actually from: Madagascar and tropical Africa

⊟ **Space, pot, and soil requirements:** Kalanchoes love drainage and aeration. They do best in a light succulent mix and a clay or terra-cotta container. Since they share similar water and light requirements, kalanchoes do well when interplanted with succulent roommates like aloes and hens and chicks.

≈ **Water requirements:** Follow the refill rule: Allow the soil to dry slightly before watering. Don't overwater it. Too much water and humidity can cause crown rot and kill kalanchoes quickly.

⩘ **Light requirements:** Kalanchoes like full sun or bright light. Stems become leggy and spindly under too little light.

☠ **Toxicity:** Toxic if eaten (cardiac glycosides)

Other tips and facts: Florist kalanchoe can bloom indoors multiple times. Flapjacks and panda plants die after flowering but can be regrown from the offsets they leave behind. Air plant kalanchoe and mother-of-thousands are especially easy to propagate from their leaf offsets. Simply remove the pups or collect them from where they've fallen, place them on top of damp potting soil, and cover with plastic wrap or a plastic bag to maintain humidity until the plantlets have grown roots.

Unlike other succulents that find fertilizer overwhelming, kalanchoes can handle their nitrogen. If they're in their own containers, you can give yours a dose of balanced fertilizer once a month in spring and summer.

Ginger

(Zingiber officinale)

Common name: Ginger

Botanical name: *Zingiber officinale*

Other names: Stem ginger, green ginger, cooking ginger, true ginger

Who it's good for: People who wanted to cook a curry three months ago and will try again in a year

Appearance: A tan rhizome sends up green pseudostems (rolled-up leaves) that unfurl into long, blade-like leaves and can reach a height of 3 to 4 feet (1 to 1.3 m).

Where you know it from: Your countertop, where it's slowly sprouting and turning pink

Where it's actually from: Tropical Asia

HOW NOT TO KILL IT

🏺 **Space, pot, and soil requirements:** Use fresh potting soil. I highly recommend splurging on a high-quality organic soil if you plan to eat your ginger. Once the ginger has leaves, put some mulch on the soil surface to help maintain moisture. Keep it at temperatures above 50°F. (10°C). When ginger gets cold, its foliage will shrivel and shed, but the rhizomes will remain alive.

≈ **Water requirements:** Give ginger a thorough soak when watering. It can't handle standing water, but it doesn't want to dry out completely.

🌤 **Light requirements:** Ginger is an understory plant in the wild, so it likes dappled light or partial shade. Keep it out of direct sunlight.

☠ **Toxicity:** Nontoxic

Other tips and facts: Your leftover ginger from the grocery store can become a beautiful houseplant once it sprouts within a few weeks. Organic ginger will likely sprout on its own, but conventional ginger is covered with sprout inhibitor and should be soaked in water overnight. To plant ginger, partially submerge sprouted rhizomes in potting mix with the buds facing up, water thoroughly, then wait. Over time, happy rhizomes will grow and expand until they fill the pot, so plan to divide, harvest, and repot ginger yearly when the stalks wither on their own.

Ginger and its cousins, turmeric and galangal, can all be grown from scraps in the same way. If you harvest the ginger at about four months while the leaves are still green, the flavor will be milder than usual. Even the ginger leaves can be chopped and used as a garnish like chive or green onion, but their flavor is distinctive. Look for recipes that call for them. Don't just start sprinkling them about, lest you waste more food that can't be turned into a houseplant.

Haworthias

(Haworthia spp. and Haworthiopsis spp.)

Common name: Haworthias

Botanical names: *Haworthia* spp. and *Haworthiopsis* spp., named for British botanist and entomologist Adrian Hardy Haworth. Haworth died tragically in the 1833 London cholera epidemic, another plague marked by denials and conspiracies ("The doctors just want your body parts!").

Other name: Zebra plant

Who it's good for: Tough, tiny people who want tough, tiny succulents

Appearance: Haworthias look like Tim Burton's aloes. Many are similar in shape, but are dark brown, red, green, or black with fuzzy white stripes or dots. These white markings are the elastic waistbands of the plant kingdom: Special pores called tubercles allow leaves to expand without tearing. Most haworthia species are tiny, reaching a maximum diameter of 3 to 6 inches (7.5 to 15 cm). Bigger specimens may just be clusters of smaller plants. Healthy, mature haworthias may send up stalks with white or pink flowers in the fall and winter (they impressively and stubbornly observe the spring and summer of their native hemisphere).

Some Haworthia species available as houseplants include:

- *H. attenuata*, known as zebra cactus, with dark green leaves and stripy bands of white tubercles
- *H. bayeri*, with dark green, flat triangular leaves and distinctive white veins
- *H. cooperi*, known as cushion aloe, with round, bubble-like leaves
- *H. fasciata*, known as zebra plant, with opaque leaves and white spots
- *H. retusa*, known as star cactus, with short, pointy, jelly-like leaves that radiate in a star shape
- *H. truncata*, known as horse's teeth, with leaves like sliced celery that spread in a linear fan instead of a circular rosette

Where you know it from: If you've seen a succulent that looked like it could be for sale at Hot Topic, it was probably a haworthia.

Where it's actually from: Most are from South Africa; others are from Namibia, Mozambique, and Swaziland.

HOW NOT TO KILL IT

🪴 **Space, pot, and soil requirements:** Haworthias are happy in a regular commercial succulent mix and pots of almost any material. Like aloes, haworthias become top-heavy, so sturdy clay pots can help them stay balanced. Unglazed and terra-cotta pots support airflow. Haworthias grow slowly and can stay in the same pot for years, but repotting them every two to three years into fresh succulent mix is good for their health.

≈ **Water requirements:** Haworthias follow the refill rule. In the summer, most haworthias will need water once a week. Counterintuitively, shriveling can indicate overwatering. While you should always drain excess water out of cachepots and saucers, root rot is not the death sentence to haworthias that it can be to other succulents. Unpot suffering haworthias, trim off slimy roots, and let them recover in the open air for a week. Repot in fresh succulent mix and water with restraint as new roots regrow.

🌤 **Light requirements:** While most succulents love sun, wild haworthias usually grow in the shade of rocks and other plants. Yours will do well in partial shade and artificial indoor lighting.

☠ **Toxicity:** Nontoxic

Other tips and facts: Europeans have been collecting haworthias since the 1600s, when colonists brought them back from southern Africa. In Japan, particularly zany haworthias with rare colors and markings can sell for several hundred dollars apiece. To propagate haworthias, gently remove the pups that grow from the base of the parent plant as soon as they have visible roots. (Please don't try selling yours to Japanese collectors, lest you run afoul of their Ministry for Agriculture.)

Hedgehog Cacti

(Echinocereus spp.)

Common name: Hedgehog cacti

Botanical name: *Echinocereus* spp. *Echinos* is an ancient Greek word for "hedgehog." *Cereus* is Latin for "candle" or "wax."

Other names: Rainbow cactus, claret cup cactus

Who it's good for: People who leave the Christmas decorations up until May and call it an "aesthetic"

Appearance: These chunky, funky cacti have a lot of personality: They're unapologetically thorny and some, like the rainbow cactus, are colorful even without flowers. Hedgehog cacti tend to be squat and cylindrical with dense, pale spines. Most are less than 12 inches (30 cm) tall, and many species have big, distinctive flowers that look like vuvuzelas. Some common hedgehog cacti you might find for sale include:

- Rainbow cactus (*Echinocereus rigidissimus* var. *rubrispinus*), which grows in clumps and has distinctive red and white bands of short spines
- Claret cup hedgehog cactus (*Echinocereus triglochidiatus*), which has deep vertical ridges, needle-like spines, and electric red flowers

- Strawberry hedgehog cactus (*Echinocereus engelmannii*), with long spines and magenta flowers

Where you know it from: Store displays around Cinco de Mayo. That's right, you can get a living ball of needles to go with your crunchy taco shells from Albertson's. These are also the most popular flowering cacti for sale. Wild strawberry hedgehogs are common across the Southwestern United States.

Where it's actually from: Arid regions of the United States, Mexico, and Central America

HOW NOT TO KILL IT

▱ **Space, pot, and soil requirements:** Use a loose, well-draining cactus or succulent soil mix. Luckily, these thorny gems like to be somewhat pot-bound and don't need frequent repotting. Once that chore becomes inevitable, use a pair of heavy leather gloves and wrap the cacti in several layers of newspaper to prevent yourself from getting stabbed. Wait several days after repotting these cacti to water them. Hedgehog cacti are comfortable at normal household temperatures but are more likely to flower if kept cooler in the winter (45°F to 55°F [7°C to 13°C]).

≈ **Water requirements:** Follow the refill rule with these cacti and let them dry slightly between waterings. In the winter, let them dry out almost completely. Give them just enough water to prevent them from shriveling.

⛅ **Light requirements:** Hedgehog cacti like bright sunlight and are happiest next to your brightest window, likely facing south or west. Don't be afraid to supplement with plenty of artificial light. These cacti grow quickly, so rotate them to prevent them from looking lumpy.

☠ **Toxicity:** Toxic if eaten (in the unlikely event that an eater can chew through the spines)

Other tips and facts: You can propagate hedgehog cacti from the pups. Carefully remove a baby hedgehog, leaving some roots attached. Let it air-dry for a few days. Once a callus has formed over the cut surface, you can give the pup its own pot of succulent mix. Keep the new plant in a warm, well-lit area and water sparingly until new growth is visible.

Hedgehog cacti contain calcium oxalates just like aroids do and are harmful if ingested, but the greatest danger is from puncture wounds. The needle-like spines can force pathogens deep into the skin, leading to painful infections that are difficult to treat and are poor candidates for a GoFundMe page, since you should have seen them coming. Keep these hazardous spike balls well out of reach of children and animals.

Hens and Chicks

(Echeveria spp. and Sempervivum spp.)

Common name: Hens and chicks

Botanical names: *Sempervivum tectorum* and *Echeveria elegans*. These two unrelated plants are known and sold as hens and chicks. The genus name *Sempervivum* is Latin for "always alive," which sets unrealistic expectations for this plant. *Tectorum* comes from *tectum*, which means "roof." The

Echeveria genus was named for Atanasio Echeverría y Godoy, an eighteenth-century naturalist and prolific botanical illustrator from Mexico.

Other names: Common houseleek (*S. tectorum*), Mexican snowball (*E. elegans*)

Who it's good for: Superstitious ancient Romans, who planted *S. tectorum* on roofs to hold shingles together and believed that this plant could prevent lightning strikes; people who did a Google image search for "succulent" and thought, "yes"

Appearance: *E. elegans* grows in a dense rosette of fleshy, pale, blue-green leaves. *S. tectorum* has a similar shape, but the leaves are flatter, with distinctive pointy tips that may be purple or red. Both plants reach about 4 inches (10 cm) in height and spread. The main rosette, the "hen," spreads via horizontal stems that develop into offsets, or "chicks." In summer, the hen sends up a stalk of flowers.

Where you know it from: The checkout counter at the Lowe's garden center; any rock garden worth its rock salt

Where it's actually from: *Sempervivum* is native to southern Europe. *Echeveria* is native to Mexico, Central America, and northwestern South America.

HOW NOT TO KILL IT

⬓ **Space, pot, and soil requirements:** Hens and chicks have shallow roots and do best in gritty, well-draining succulent mixes. Long, shallow containers with plenty of drainage holes work best.

≈ **Water requirements:** Err on the side of underwatering. Think root rot is gross? Hens and chicks are also prone to *crown* rot, so follow the refill rule.

✿ Light requirements: Hens and chicks do best with at least three to four hours a day of full sun or bright light, but they tolerate partial shade.

☠ Toxicity: *S. tectorum* is mildly toxic (alkaloids). *E. elegans* is nontoxic.

Other tips and facts: When it comes to propagation, think of the chicks as college-bound teens instead of babies, and don't be afraid to remove them. The hen aspires to be an empty nester: So much of the parent plant's energy supports the chicks that it benefits from their removal. Once a *Sempervivum*'s flowers set seed, the hen dies, leaving the chicks to spread. Don't let this deter you from adding these plants to your collection. Many specimens produce chicks for years before flowering, and some *Echeveria* hens can flower multiple times before they decline.

Hens and chicks dislike fertilizer. They're adapted to growing in rocky soils and cracks in walls. Too much nitrogen will make them soft and prone to rot, which is deadly in combination with overwatering.

Jade Plant

(Crassula ovata)

Common name: Jade plant

Botanical names: *Crassula ovata, Crassula argentea.* The word *crassula* is Latin for "fat" or "thick." *Ovata* means "egg-shaped."

Other names: Baby jade, Japanese rubber plant

Who it's good for: People who want a plant that looks plastic but is actually real, instead of the other way around; people who want to tinker and fuss over a succulent bonsai tree

Appearance: Jade plants have multiple woody stems bearing clusters of fleshy, shiny, dark green, egg-shaped leaves at the ends of their branches. The leaves are about 1 to 3 inches (2 to 7.5 cm) long and develop a red edge in sufficient sunlight. Mature plants can reach up to 5 feet (1.5 m) in height and produce star-shaped pink or white flowers in winter. The bark of mature plants peels away in horizontal strips.

Some of the many jade plant varieties you may find include:

- 'Variegata', with creamy stripes
- 'Tricolor', a miniature variety with pink and white streaks
- The adorable bonsai 'Hobbit'
- 'Gollum', with finger-like, tubular leaves
- The psychedelic 'Hummel's Sunset', which has Gollum-shaped foliage and ombre leaves with bright green bases and electric-red tips

Where you know it from: This one looks like a tree made out of Jordan almonds and is an alarmingly picked-over specimen at the botanical garden

Where it's actually from: South Africa and Mozambique. *C. ovata* is common across South Africa's Eastern Cape.

HOW NOT TO KILL IT

🪴 **Space, pot, and soil requirements:** Jade plants have small root systems but can become very heavy as they grow. A sturdy clay or ceramic pot is ideal. These plants do well if repotted every two to three years, but you can keep them smaller by leaving them in smaller pots longer. Jade plants like dry air and are unlikely to bloom in high humidity.

≈ **Water requirements:** Water your jade plant when the top 1 inch (2.5 cm) of soil is dry. Give it a good soak, then drain off any remaining water from the saucer or cachepot. Underwatered jade plants will shrivel and drop leaves. Overwatered jade plants may show signs of edema: blisters that turn into brown, cork-like spots.

☀ **Light requirements:** Jade plants tolerate partial shade and love full sun. If you move a jade plant from a darker to a sunnier spot in your home, expose the plant to brighter light gradually to prevent sunburn.

☠ **Toxicity:** Toxic if eaten (severe vomiting and dizziness)

Other tips and facts: These are tortoises among houseplants (though infinitely less likely to give you salmonella): If you succeed in caring for your jade plant, it can live for over a hundred years. Originally from the Cape of South Africa, jade plants and geraniums were some of the first plants that the Dutch settlers brought back to Europe. The Khoi and other Indigenous peoples ate the roots and used the leaves for medicine. Your jade plant is for decorative use only.

Jade plants appreciate a good spring haircut. Trimming off the smallest branches encourages the plant to grow stronger roots and helps the plant support the weight of its luscious leaves. If you want a bonsai succulent, jade plants are a great choice, because they can be sculpted into unique shapes and are easy to keep small.

Unfortunately, mealybugs go nuts for jade plants. Try wiping them off with a cotton swab dipped in alcohol. Avoid insecticidal soap and products that contain it, as it can damage the foliage.

If you love jade plants, look for their rounder, paler blue cousins, silver dollar plants (*Crassula arborescens*), that require similar care.

Lucky Bamboo

(Dracaena sanderiana)

Common name: Lucky bamboo

Botanical name: *Dracaena sanderiana*. The genus name comes from *drakaina*, a Greek word for "female dragon," and the species is named after Henry Frederick Conrad Sander (1847–1920), the Victorian era's leading orchid collector, hybridizer, and illustrator.

Other names: Ribbon plant, friendship bamboo

Who it's good for: Feng shui enthusiasts; people who like the look of bamboo but understand that the world's fastest growing plant is a poor choice for indoor containers

Appearance: Lucky bamboo may look like bamboo, but there's no relation. Bamboo is a grass, and technically this plant is an asparagus (DO NOT EAT). Lucky bamboo has thin, upright stems with clear nodes and thin, bright green, lance-shaped leaves up to 7 inches (18 cm) long. The stems are often trained into braids, spirals, and other shapes, held in place with gold foil twist ties. Mature plants can reach up to 5 feet (1.5 m) in height and spread, but most plants for sale are very small and can be pruned to maintain their size.

Where you know it from: Asian gift shops and supermarkets. This plant is next to the Lucky Cat and the Samurai swords of dubious provenance (eBay? The Renaissance festival?) on your white ex-boyfriend's mantlepiece.

Where it's actually from: Cameroon and tropical western Africa

HOW NOT TO KILL IT

⊟ **Space, pot, and soil requirements:** This plant can grow in regular potting mix, or in water with pebbles to anchor the roots.

≈ **Water requirements:** While lucky bamboo can grow in water, it doesn't tolerate waterlogged soil. If your plant is in soil, water regularly to keep it damp, but not swampy. If your plant is in water and pebbles, change the water weekly and give it a tiny, weak dose of liquid fertilizer.

⚶ **Light requirements:** Lucky bamboo likes partial shade and indirect light, and it tolerates almost complete darkness. Keep this plant vampire out of the sun. Direct light will scorch the leaves.

☠ **Toxicity:** Mildly toxic if eaten (saponins)

Other tips and facts: Dry conditions, too much light, or chlorine in the water can cause the leaf tips to turn brown. Using filtered water can help.

Lucky bamboo is easy to propagate from stem cuttings. Using a clean, sharp knife, simply trim a stem with at least two nodes at an angle, just above a node. Remove the bottom leaves, stick the cut end into pebbles for stability, and fill the container with water. Change the water weekly.

Miniature Date Palm

(Phoenix roebelenii)

Common name:
Miniature date palm

Botanical name:
Phoenix roebelenii

Other names: The politically
incorrect Pygmy date palm
and dwarf date palm

Who it's good for: Friends of
the frond who can keep a kentia

palm alive and want something with more texture and personality

Appearance: Miniature date palms have slender trunks covered in stubbly old leaf bases. These palms are individualists whose trunks often grow curved instead of straight. The leaves and crown have a classic palm shape: The trunk ends in a dense cluster of feather-shaped, arching leaves with narrow leaflets. Mature, outdoor trees flower in the spring, and female trees bear edible dates. Mature trees can reach a height of 12 feet (4 m) and a spread of 6 to 8 feet (2 to 2.5 m).

Where you know it from: If you've been to Florida, you've seen it in someone's yard. This is the state's most popular small landscape palm.

Where it's actually from: Southern central China, Laos, Myanmar, Thailand, and Vietnam, especially along the banks of the Mekong River

HOW NOT TO KILL IT

🏺 **Space, pot, and soil requirements:** Soil drainage is key. Fortunately, this palm doesn't need frequent repotting. It prefers to be somewhat root-bound. Keep this plant away from doorways in winter, because it doesn't tolerate drafts of cold air well.

≈ **Water requirements:** Keep the soil slightly moist during the spring and summer. Miniature date palms are prone to root rot, so don't overwater them. Established palms can tolerate a moderate amount of drought (neglect).

🌿 **Light requirements:** The miniature date palm likes bright, indirect light but needs protection from intense, full sun. An east-facing window is its happy place. If your mini-date palm is young and doesn't have a visible trunk yet, don't mistake it for a kentia and leave it in the dark.

☠ Toxicity: Nontoxic

Other tips and facts: Watch out for mealybugs and scale. However, what looks like light-colored scale on new leaves is probably just scurf: whitish, slightly raised, elongated, waxy spots that run parallel to the midribs of fronds and leaflets. These spots are completely normal and fall off as the fronds mature. Check for shiny, sticky honeydew to tell the difference.

Prune off dead or dying outer leaves with a sharp, clean blade. To encourage fresh fronds, give this palm a diluted (one-quarter strength) dose of all-purpose liquid fertilizer two or three times during spring and summer.

Money Tree

(*Pachira aquatica*)

Common name: Money tree

Botanical name: *Pachira aquatica*. *Pachira* is the plant's native Guayanese name, and *aquatica* indicates that it grows in or near water.

Other names: Guiana chestnut, Malabar chestnut, water chestnut. Don't confuse this plant with the water chestnuts used in Asian cuisine. Those are tubers from the *Eleocharis dulcis* plant, native to China. The name "money tree" comes from a folktale: A poor man found the tree, began selling the seeds, and became wealthy. The money tree is said to bring luck to homes and offices, but do not buy this plant if you are trying to "manifest" money: You will only manifest a little bit more credit card debt.

Who it's good for: Plant owners who are willing to water and who squeal with joy at the sight of a NEW BABY LEAF. New leaves on this plant look like tiny green hands reaching up to high-five you for keeping them alive.

Appearance: In the wild, these broadleaf evergreen trees can reach up to 60 feet (18 m) tall with a 30-foot (10 m) spread. Each leaf has five to nine pointy leaflets between 5 and 10 inches (12 and 25 cm) long. Feeling pressure to reproduce? These trees empathize. Outdoors, they bloom for a single day. Your money tree houseplant is unlikely to flower. Most indoor money trees are braided bonsais held together with twist ties. As a houseplant, a money tree can reach up to 6 to 8 feet (2 to 2.5 m).

Where you know it from: The danger zone at Ikea between the showroom and the warehouse. It's your last impulse purchase before the cinnamon rolls.

Where it's actually from: Riverbanks and freshwater swamps in the tropical rainforests of northern South America and Mexico. It's also grown outdoors in Southern California and Hawai'i.

HOW NOT TO KILL IT

⊟ **Space, pot, and soil requirements:** A bonsai version will be comfortable for a while in the pot it came in. If you want a bigger money tree (remember, it *will not* bring you bigger money), repot it annually.

≈ **Water requirements:** Keep the soil consistently damp, but not soaked. A money tree can tolerate wet soil in a pot with great drainage. Otherwise, it may turn yellow or develop root rot. This species draws the line at dry soil and will begin to drop shriveled leaves that look like the indignant hands of the betrayed.

☈ **Light requirements:** This lucky little tree isn't fussy. It likes full sun to partial shade, but can tolerate close to full shade. It does best in bright light.

☠ **Toxicity:** Nontoxic

> **Other tips and facts:** In ideal outdoor conditions, mature money trees develop 12-inch (30 cm) capsules with large, edible seeds that can be eaten raw or roasted.

Philodendrons

(Philodendron spp. and Thaumatophyllum bipinnatifidum)

Philodendrons form a diverse group, including tree and vine types. Popular houseplant species include the tree philodendron (*Thaumatophyllum bipinnatifidum*), the shrubby-looking red leaf philodendron (*Philodendron erubescens*), elephant ear philodendrons (*Philodendron giganteum*), and the trailing heartleaf vine (*Philodendron hederaceum*).

Common name: Philodendrons

Botanical names: *Philodendron* is Greek for "tree lover," referring to the genus's many tree-climbing species. Tree philodendron is *Thaumatophyllum bipinnatifidum,* but its previous names, *Philodendron bipinnatifidum* and *Philodendron selloum*, are still commonly used, so you know it gets at least six copies of the L.L. Bean catalog. *Thaumatophyllum* is Greek for "miraculous leaf."

Other names: Tree philodendron is also known as lacy tree philodendron, horsehead philodendron, and fiddle-leaf philodendron. Heartleaf may also be called sweetheart plant, parlor ivy, or my personal favorite: vilevine.

Who it's good for: Tree philodendrons with lots of aerial roots will thrill devotees of the Flying Spaghetti Monster. The pink princess variegated philodendron is good for people who post a lot of selfies and selectively listen to music with their Spotify Wrapped in mind all year.

Appearance: Tree philodendrons develop a single, unbranched, woody trunk up to 4 inches (10 cm) thick that sends out ropy aerial roots. The youngest leaves are heart shaped. Mature leaves can reach 30 inches (75 cm) and grow on petioles (leaf stems) up to 3 feet (1 m) long. Mature leaves are arrowhead shaped and divided into deep, distinctive lobes with wavy edges. In the wild, tree philodendrons climb tall trees in search of better light. A popular dwarf variety is the *Philodendron* 'Xanadu' hybrid.

Heartleaf is the most common philodendron houseplant. Its long stems have dark green, heart-shaped leaves about 5 inches (12 cm) long. In the wild, heartleaf is less altruistic than its name suggests: It climbs tree trunks and absorbs nutrients and moisture from the bark.

Red leaf and elephant ear philodendrons are slow climbers that look shrubby as houseplants. Their elongated, heart-shaped leaves can reach up to 16 inches (40 cm). The red leaf philodendron actually has dark green leaves with coppery undersides and pink or red petioles (leaf stems). 'Pink Princess' is a popular but divisive cultivar.

Where you know it from:
Heartleaf philodendron is the pothos that *won't* make your cat ralph all over the sofa. Tree philodendrons are common landscape plants in Florida and coastal Georgia. The SUPER-RARE PINK PRINCESS VARIEGATED PHILODENDRON is all over the internet and fetches outrageous prices. (Beware: Scammers use gases to produce hormones that temporarily render ordinary foliage pink. If you're into this trend, buy your plants from a reputable source.)

Where it's actually from:
The tree philodendron is from southeastern Brazil and Paraguay. Heartleaf is from Mexico and Central and South America. The red leaf philodendron is from Colombia, and the elephant ear philodendron is from the Caribbean.

HOW NOT TO KILL IT

⊟ **Space, pot, and soil requirements:** All philodendrons like rich soil with good drainage. Tree philodendrons are alarmingly robust growers. To keep yours from crawling out of its pot and moving into the guest room, trim off some outer roots and repot it back into its original container. Trailing heartleaf does well in a hanging basket or raised pot, but it can also be trained to climb a post like monstera. All philodendrons like to stay warm (above 65°F [18°C]).

≈ **Water requirements:** Keep philodendrons consistently damp without letting the soil become swampy. Wild philodendrons grow along riverbanks, so they like water. Overwatered philodendrons turn yellow and drop leaves. Philodendrons do best with high humidity, so give them a regular mist with a spray bottle. You can also nestle philodendrons in snugly with other (healthy, pest-free) houseplants to keep the humidity higher around them.

🌤 **Light requirements:** Philodendrons prefer partial shade or filtered sunlight, but artificial light is fine. These plants can tolerate low light for a long time, especially heartleaf. Philodendrons kept in the dark will develop spindly stems and smaller leaves with fewer lobes.

☠ **Toxicity:** Heartleaf is pet safe. Other philodendrons are toxic if eaten. The sap is irritating to skin and eyes, so wear gloves and goggles when pruning or repotting.

Other tips and facts: Philodendrons are heavy feeders that like regular doses of balanced fertilizer in spring and summer.

Wild tree philodendrons literally heat things up when it comes to pollination. When it first opens, the flower rises to 18°F (10°C) above the ambient air temperature. By nightfall, the blossom can reach 95°F to 115°F (35°C to 46°C). Supposedly, the heat releases an attractive odor reminiscent of vanilla, cinnamon, and black pepper. Within two hours, the plant attracts hundreds of scarab beetle pollinators. (Since philodendrons are unlikely to flower indoors, if you're trying to attract scarabs, it's much more efficient to anger an Egyptian god.)

Spider Plant

(Chlorophytum comosum)

Common name: Spider plant

Botanical name: *Chlorophytum comosum*. The genus name is impressively uncreative: It comes from *chloros*, the Greek word for "green," and *phyton*, meaning "plant." The species name, *comosum*, means "furnished with a tuft."

Other names: Ribbon plant, spider ivy, airplane plant

Who it's good for: People who still want to use those

hanging macramé planters, even though the begonia, croton, and maidenhair fern all died in there

Appearance: Spider plants have long, thin leaves with a lengthwise ridge that originate out from the plant's center. The "parent" plants usually max out at about 12 to 15 inches (30 to 38 cm). Spider plants send out long stems called stolons that can reach up to 2 feet (60 cm) and may produce tiny, white, star-shaped flowers. Pollinated flowers yield capsules with black, flat seeds. Regardless of pollination (unlikely in your home, unless you have bees for some reason), once the flowers are gone, the "spiders" (baby plantlets) develop at the end of stems. The 'Variegatum' cultivar has green leaves with white edges, and the 'Vittatum' cultivar has white leaves with green edges.

Where you know it from: Many a fluorescent-lit office. I know this plant from my dentist's office, where it shrugs at me casually from the window as if to say, "What, you want a prize for flossing?"

Where it's actually from: Coastal South Africa

HOW NOT TO KILL IT

⊟ **Space, pot, and soil requirements:** Spider plants are happiest in hanging baskets. Repotting is a minor conundrum. These plants are fast growers with tough roots that can break containers, especially plastic pots. It's good to divide and repot your spider plants once things get tight. However, spider plants grow and produce plantlets the fastest when they're a little bit pot-bound.

≈ **Water requirements:** Allow the soil to dry slightly between waterings. When you water, water deeply over a sink or bathtub. Spider plants tolerate dry air and soil but will turn brown at the tips if they're too dry. They appreciate the occasional mist from a spray bottle during the summer. Fluoride and chlorine in tap water can also cause leaf burn. If using distilled or bottled water is unrealistic (I mean, do *you* even drink water?), letting a container of tap water sit out overnight before watering will at least allow the chlorine to dissipate.

🌿 **Light requirements:** Spider plants like bright, indirect light. They can tolerate heavy shade, but not direct sunlight. They'll scorch and fade in bright sun. Spider plants do especially well in artificial light, making them a great choice for the drop-tile ceiling crowd. Root and plantlet growth is dependent on day length. If the parent plant receives short days (less than twelve hours of light) and long nights (uninterrupted darkness) for at least three weeks, you will start seeing spider plantlets *fast*.

☠ **Toxicity:** Mildly toxic

> **Other tips and facts:** Want more spiders? Hold off on the fertilizer. Spider plants' tubers store food and overfertilized plants are less likely to produce baby plantlets. Dividing is one way to propagate these prodigious plants. The other is by planting the "mature" spiders that develop roots while still attached to the parent. These can be trimmed off and transferred to their own pots.
>
> The hanging plantlets are attractive to cats, who may like to play with them and chew on them. For a pet-safe alternative, try heartleaf philodendron or a hanging Boston fern.
>
> Even healthy spider plants will have yellow leaves and some brown tips. Just prune those off.

Umbrella Trees

(Schefflera actinophylla and Schefflera arboricola)

Common names: Umbrella tree and dwarf umbrella plant

Botanical names: The umbrella tree is *Schefflera actinophylla*, named for its radiating leaflets. The dwarf umbrella plant is *Schefflera arboricola*. *Arboricola* means "tree-like." The genus is named after Johann Peter Ernst von Scheffler, a doctor, botanist, alchemist, freemason, and all-around overachieving mystery man of nineteenth-century Poland.

Other names: Australian ivy palm (it's neither an ivy nor a palm), starleaf, octopus tree

Who it's good for: Homesick Queenslanders; people who meant to buy a money tree and picked up this little cosplayer instead

Appearance: Umbrella tree leaves have distinctive, oblong leaflets that radiate outward in a circle, like the ribs of an umbrella. In the wild, the dwarf umbrella tree can reach 25 feet (8 m) tall and sometimes grows in the branches of other trees as an epiphyte (a benevolent parasite that only needs lodging). Your houseplant version is unlikely to top 6 feet (2 m). The umbrella tree is bigger all around. It can reach 50 feet (15 m) in the wild (up to 15 feet [5 m] in your home) and also has more leaflets than its little cousin, up to sixteen per leaf. The nickname "octopus tree" doesn't mean that Australians can't count. It refers to the plant's funky flowers that look like purple tentacles. Sadly, you're unlikely to ever see these on your houseplant.

Where you know it from: Your college roommate's desk, where it was positioned to drop its dying leaves straight into the trash can

Where it's actually from: The dwarf umbrella plant is from Hainan and Taiwan and the umbrella tree is from Australia and New Guinea. You might see an umbrella tree in southern Florida or Hawai'i, where it's an invasive species.

HOW NOT TO KILL IT

⬱ **Space, pot, and soil requirements:** All these plants ask for is good drainage. Keep these plants above 60°F (16°C) in the winter.

≈ **Light requirements:** These plants like partial shade and are especially happy next to windows with light-filtering curtains. About three to four hours of sunlight a day is ideal, so about the same minimum that keeps humans from descending into madness. Avoid direct sunlight.

🌤 **Water requirements:** During spring and summer, water these umbrellas regularly without drowning them. Back off a bit during winter. Allow the soil to nearly dry between waterings. Both of these species will drop leaves if the soil is too dry OR too moist, just like my nemesis, the trendy and capricious fiddle leaf fig (*Ficus lyrata*, not profiled). If you're using a spray bottle to mist other, more sensitive plants, give these umbrellas an occasional mist as well.

☠ **Toxicity:** Low toxicity. Safe for cats and dogs.

> **Other tips and facts:** As with pothos and other glossy-leaved plants, you may need to dust these.
>
> Prune off any leaves that turn yellow. Even the dwarf umbrella plant can grow vigorously, so be prepared to do some pruning to keep its size under control.

Fussy
Houseplants

Air Plants

(Tillandsia spp.)

Common names: Air plants, tillandsias

Botanical names: *Tillandsia* spp. The genus was named for Swedish botanist and medical professor Elias Tillandz, who changed his surname from Tillander after surviving a shipwreck. *Til lands* is Swedish for "ashore." Ironically, one of the best ways to water his namesake plants is to submerge them.

Other names: Ball moss, needle leaf

Who it's good for: People who refer to chotchkes as *objets*; people who like to reward their decluttering efforts with a little trip to HomeGoods; people able and willing to make air plant care a daily or weekly task

Appearance: Air plants look like pineapple crowns: rosettes of stiff leaves that range from tight and spiky to long and curly. They use their roots to attach to other plants, rocks, or surfaces and absorb all water and nutrients from the atmosphere using structures called trichomes. Happy air plants may send forth small pink, purple, or red blossoms from their centers. Once air plants flower, they die off, but not without sending up new pups in their place.

"Mesic" air plants (which grow in moderate moisture) are dark green with smooth, cupped leaves. These species come from darker, humid rainforests. Species include:

- *T. butzii*, with purplish foliage and tentacle-like leaves
- *T. bulbosa*, with onion-shaped bases that house ant colonies in the wild
- *T. aeranthos bergeri*, known as the "Mad Pupper," which forms dense, spherical clusters
- *T. flabellata*, with smooth, colorful leaves

"Xeric" air plants (which grow in dry conditions) are the gray, fuzzy species that come from deserts and usually grow on rocks. Their silvery sheen reflects sunlight, keeping them cooler and reducing their water needs. Species include:

- *T. pruinosa*, known as the "Fuzzy Wuzzy" air plant, native to Florida
- *T. streptophylla*, called "Shirley Temple" for its tight, curly leaves
- *T. baileyi*, known as "Giant Ball Moss," native to southern Texas
- *T. brachycaulos*, whose leaves turn electric pink and purple as it comes into bloom

These fuzzy ones may be easier to care for because they can tolerate sporadic and neglectful watering.

Where you know it from:
Those zany glass bubbles at West Elm. You may also have seen ball moss growing on fences, telephone wires, or other structures in South Florida or Texas. Spanish moss (*Tillandsia usneoides*), which hangs from trees along the coastal southern United States, is also an air plant, though it's more commonly used as a mulch than a houseplant.

Where it's actually from:
All over the tropical and subtropical Americas

HOW NOT TO KILL IT

⊟ **Space, pot, and soil requirements:** The possibilities for air plant containers are almost endless. They can be grown in rocks, among shells, on bark or branches, in open terrariums, on macramé contraptions, or hung from the ceiling with wire or fishing line. Heck, you could even scalp a troll doll and give it botanical hair. What matters most is that the container does not hold any water.

≈ **Water requirements:** There are several ways to water air plants. The best way is the one you will actually make time for and remember to do.

- Soaking: Once a week, remove your air plants from their containers and submerge them in room-temperature water for twenty to thirty minutes. Gently shake the plants to remove moisture from the inside of the leaves. Then, allow them to finish drying upside down for several hours before returning them to a container to prevent them from rotting. If your air plants get crispy edges despite regular dunking, allow the container of water to sit out overnight before you give them their bath: Chlorine in the tap water will dissipate.

- Rinsing: Twice a week, run your air plants under a faucet with lukewarm water, then gently shake and drain facedown on a paper towel.

- Misting: Every other day, give your air plants a few diffuse spritzes from a spray bottle. If your air plants are dark green and smooth, or if the humidity in your home is very low, they may need more than just a spritz. The darker the color and smoother the leaves, the more water your air plant will need. Underwatered air plants will signal their distress with dull, tightly curled, crispy leaves that may develop brown tips.

🌿 **Light requirements:** Air plants need bright, indirect light. Keep them close to a window, but out of harsh, direct sun. The lighter the plant, the more sunlight it can handle.

☠ **Toxicity:** Nontoxic

Other tips and facts: However you choose to display your air plants, beware of trendy copper wire. The residue on oxidized copper (the green-and-white gunk on old pennies) is toxic to air plants. (Copper fungicides are used to kill ball moss on commercial pecan trees.) Some workarounds include making sure the copper wire is coated or sealed, removing the plants for watering and only returning them once they're *completely* dry, and using fake copper products instead (painted or made of brass). The prettiest copper fixture on all of Etsy will look like garbage if it's full of dead tillandsias.

You can give your air plants a bromeliad fertilizer once a month. When soaking the plants, dilute the fertilizer to one-quarter of the dosage listed on the package and add it to the water. Drain and dry as usual.

To propagate your air plants, gently remove the pups that emerge at the base after flowering. Once those babies are a third of the parent plant's size, give them their own troll doll/ glass bubble/wire contraption: They are mature enough to grow on their own.

If you're in an area where air plants grow in the wild, be sure to buy your air plants from nurseries instead of harvesting them. Overcollection has endangered many native populations. Threatening biodiversity just to add some whimsy to your terrarium is indefensibly tacky.

Avocado Tree
(Persea americana)

Common name: Avocado

Botanical name:
Persea americana

Other names: Alligator pear. The name "avocado" comes from from a Nahuatl word that is also Aztec slang for testicle, which is the last thing I want to think about while I'm destroying various industries and the housing market by enjoying my generation's favorite breakfast food.

Who it's good for: Patient avocado eaters who don't have cats or dogs in the house; anyone still bitter about not getting a medal at their elementary school science fair

Appearance: Avocado trees can have multiple stems and reach up to 60 feet (18 m) in the wild. The leaves are usually between 4 and 8 inches (10 to 20 cm) long, glossy dark green, with pointed tips. Tiny yellow-green flowers bloom in compound clusters called panicles. Your homegrown avocado tree may flower within several years, but don't get out the toaster or the big stone mortar just yet. Homegrown trees are unlikely to bear fruit.

Where you know it from: The gift to humanity that is Mexican food; generational culture war think pieces from the late 2010s

Where it's actually from: Avocado trees are native to south-central Mexico, Central America, and South America. A small percentage of avocados eaten in the United States come from southern Florida (the smoother, greener varieties), but the majority are dark, wrinkly Hass avocados grown in Southern California. "Hass" is also the German word for hatred. Anyone who's missed the ripeness mark and topped a salad with what taste like cubes of bar soap or dipped a tortilla chip into gray slime will question the coincidence.

HOW NOT TO KILL IT

⬒ **Space, pot, and soil requirements:** Fresh pits should be planted with two-thirds of the pit under evenly damp soil, broad-side down. A 6-inch (10 cm) diameter pot is ideal. The pit should begin to grow roots within two weeks and send up leaves within six weeks. Once new avocado seedlings reach a height of 12 to 16 inches (30 to 40 cm), they can be repotted.

If you only take away one piece of information from this book, may it be this: Plant your avocado pits in soil. An avocado pit suspended in water with toothpicks has an abysmally low chance of sprouting and a 100 percent chance of looking like Sputnik in a urine sample.

≈ **Water requirements:** Avocados like a moderate amount of water. They're happy when damp, but are prone to root rot if they stay saturated.

⚡ **Light requirements:** Once established, these babies need full sun. Seedlings grown from pits do well in indirect light.

☠ **Toxicity:** Avocado trees are toxic to pets. Choosing between dogs and avocados is millennial torture.

Other tips and facts: While homegrown avocado trees won't bring you a harvest, they're a fun way to recycle food scraps and get cute, tropical houseplants for free (or for the cost of soil and pots). I like to give them as gifts. They're the adult version of macaroni art: hard to exchange and not what anyone asked for, but the effort is endearing.

If you're ambitious and want to grow your avocado trees faster, you can try this fancy horticultural method:

- Soak a fresh avocado pit in hot water (106°F to 130°F [40°C to 52°C]) for thirty minutes.

- Slice the top ½ inch (1 cm) off of the narrow end with a sharp, clean knife.

- Dip the cut surface in a sulfur-based fungicide powder, such as Bonide.

- Plant the pit in damp seedling mix with the top just above the soil surface. Keep moist.

- Look for signs of germination in four weeks.

Bird's Nest Fern

(Asplenium nidus)

Common name: Bird's nest fern

Botanical name: *Asplenium nidus*. The *Asplenium* genus is also known as the spleenworts. Its name comes from a Greek term meaning "without a spleen," based on the Doctrine of Signatures, an age-old pseudoscience (still espoused by forwarded emails and grainy Pinterest posts) that claims that plants treat conditions related to the human organs they resemble. The species name *nidus* refers to the fern's nest-like shape.

Other names: Fettuccini fern, "The florist was out of orchids"

Who it's good for: Classy burnouts whose Pelotons are now very fancy clothes racks; people with a window in the bathroom (winning at life in New York City or crashing at home in the 'burbs)

Appearance: Bird's nest ferns have bright green, strap-shaped fronds with wavy margins and dark brown to black midribs. On the undersides of the fronds, sori (clusters of spore-producing structures, pronounced "sore-eye") appear in a herringbone-like pattern of short, straight lines. In the wild, bird's nest ferns grow as epiphytes on trees and mossy surfaces as well as in the soil. The fronds form a nest-shaped rosette that catches fallen leaves and other organic matter, which nourish the plant. Fronds on mature, outdoor plants can reach up to 5 feet (1.5 m) in length, while fronds on indoor houseplants max out at 2 feet (60 cm). Dozens of cultivars are available as houseplants, including miniatures and varieties with forked or lobed frond tips.

Where you know it from: The flower and gift section at Whole Foods (it's a very fancy fern)

Where it's actually from: Bird's nest fern has a wide native range that spans from Madagascar to Southeast Asia, Australia, Hawai'i, and Polynesia.

HOW NOT TO KILL IT

⊟ **Space, pot, and soil requirements:** Bird's nest ferns do well in regular potting soil and need good drainage. If your fern begins to outgrow its container, repot it in spring as soon as it begins to put forth new fronds. Although they have tropical origins, bird's nest ferns have come to love central air. They're happiest between 60°F and 70°F (15°C and 20°C). Drafts and direct heat can cause the fronds to turn brown at the edges.

≈ **Water requirements:** Keep bird's nest ferns' soil consistently damp and keep the humidity around them high by misting with a spray bottle. If your bathroom has a window, this fern calls dibs on it. Just be sure not to let water collect in the center of the fern, the "crown."

Light requirements: Stay away from extremes. Bird's nest ferns dislike direct sun and full shade. Try placing your fern by a window that doesn't face south or in another well-lit area of your home.

Toxicity: Nontoxic

Other tips and facts: Handle with care! This plant has fragile foliage. If you see scale or mealybugs, stick to horticultural soaps if pest treatment escalates beyond gentle excoriation. Chemical insecticides will damage the fronds.

Boston Fern

(Nephrolepis exaltata)

Common name: Boston fern

Botanical name: *Nephrolepis exaltata* 'Bostoniensis'

Other names: Fluffy ruffles, sword fern

Who it's good for: People who want to give the Roomba something to do

Appearance: Boston ferns grow in dense, fluffy clusters of feather-like fronds up to 4 feet (1.5 m) in length with alternating, serrated leaflets. Two rows of round sori (spore-bearing organs) line the undersides. Unlike many ferns, which only reproduce using spores, Boston ferns spread like spider plants: Long, thin stolons extend from the plant and develop into new ferns when they touch soil. For a smaller plant that tolerates a darker or drier environment, try the 'Dallas Jewel' cultivar. For a thick, puffy fern that looks like a Muppet, try 'Fluffy Duffy'.

Where you know it from: Hanging baskets on front porches across the United States, from humble suburban ranch houses to the buck-wild New Orleans French Quarter

Where it's actually from: Forests from Florida to northern South America

HOW NOT TO KILL IT

⊟ **Space, pot, and soil requirements:** Your Boston fern will do best in a basket or in a raised container that lets its long fronds hang down. These ferns also appreciate cooler temperatures than most tropical plants. If you enjoy sleeping in cave-like temperatures (below 70°F [20°C]), let your Boston fern move into the bedroom.

≈ **Water requirements:** Water Boston ferns over a sink or bathtub to give them a thorough soak and keep their soil consistently moist. Hanging them near a bathroom or kitchen gives them a humidity boost and makes watering more convenient. If they dry out, you'll be sweeping up huge piles of crispy brown leaflets. If your home is especially dry, give these ferns a regular spritz with a spray bottle. However, be careful in winter: When ferns go dormant, they're susceptible to root rot.

🌿 **Light requirements:** Boston ferns like bright, indirect light. They'll be happy in an east-facing window or slightly offset from a south-facing window. Avoid direct sunlight: Again, you risk the crisp.

☠ **Toxicity:** Nontoxic

Other tips and facts: Guess who "went to school in Boston": This botanical humblebragger was discovered in Cambridge, Massachusetts, in 1894. One plant in a shipment of ferns from Philadelphia was growing faster than others and had impressively arching foliage. The florist propagated it, and it soon became a darling of the Victorian horticultural trade.

Bromeliads

(Bromeliaceae)

Common name: Bromeliads

Botanical names: Commonly available genera include urn plants (*Aechmea*), pineapples (*Ananas*), earth stars (*Cryptanthus*), living vases (*Guzmania*), fingernail plants (*Neoregelia*), and vrieseas (*Vriesea*).

Other names: Dart frog starter homes

Who it's good for: Fans of air plants ready to try their trickier terrestrial cousins; greener-thumbed enthusiasts willing to learn more about their houseplant species' specific daily needs

Appearance: Bromeliads grow in symmetrical rosettes of stiff leaves, often with a colorful flower stalk emerging from the center (especially urn plants and vrieseas). Many species (urn plants, living vases, and fingernail plants) also hold water and debris in a "tank" at the center of the rosette that delivers additional water and nutrients to the plant. Bromeliads can be epiphytic (growing on trees or rocks) or terrestrial (growing out of the ground) and can range in height from 1 inch (2.5 cm) to 3 feet (1 m). Foliage colors, patterns, and textures vary dramatically.

Where you know it from: If you've ever seen a pineapple, you've seen a bromeliad (a teachable moment no one asked for on Piña Colada night). If you've ever seen a plant with a flower that looked like a chandelier made of Barbie shoes, it was probably an *Aechmea* (urn plant). Small bromeliads are popular in terrariums.

Where it's actually from: Tropical regions of North and South America. The pineapple species we eat, *Ananas comosus*, comes from Paraguay and southern Brazil (strike two on Piña Colada night).

HOW NOT TO KILL IT

⊟ **Space, pot, and soil requirements:** All bromeliads prefer pots on the smaller side. They have small root systems, and pots that are too big hold excess water. If a bromeliad is too top-heavy in a pot that fits, place that pot into a larger, sturdier cachepot. Drainage is imperative: Even the most tropical, moisture-loving bromeliads need airflow.

≈ **Water requirements:** Follow the refill rule: Give your bromeliad a good drink, then allow the soil to mostly dry before watering again. It's better to err on the side of dryness because these plants are so prone to root rot. (The smell of a dying bromeliad will *never* leave you. Regularly check the soil to spare yourself.) Moist air, however, is welcome. Regularly mist your bromeliad with a spray bottle.

Tank bromeliads require some special attention. The tank should be full of water at all times, but be careful not to drench the soil while refilling it. It's a good idea to "flush the tank" every once in a while by rinsing it out with fresh water. This prevents mineral buildup and stagnant sludge.

⚶ **Light requirements:** Bromeliads like it bright, but keep them out of harsh, direct sun. Fluorescent indoor light is totally fine. Like air plants, the darker and softer the bromeliad's foliage, the less light it needs. Bleaching, yellowing foliage indicates too much light, while soft, dark, drooping leaves indicate too little. The brighter the light, the higher humidity the plant will need.

☠ **Toxicity:** Nontoxic

Other tips and facts: Bromeliads slowly die after flowering but grow pups at the base. Once these offsets are a third of the size of the parent plant, they can be removed and repotted. Keep newly repotted pups in partial shade, DRY soil, and high humidity until the roots begin to grow. You can propagate pineapples by slicing off the "topknot" of the fruit and planting it directly into fresh soil (I am no longer invited to Piña Colada night).

Love this plant baby? Splurge on a special bromeliad fertilizer (also great for air plants [*Tillandsia*]) or a fertilizer for acid-loving plants. Dilute to one-quarter of the recommended strength and apply regularly during spring and summer.

Citrus Trees

(*Citrus spp.*)

Common name: Citrus

Botanical names: The citrus we find in grocery stores are nearly all hybrids of hybrids of hybrids, remixed over the years for maximum flavor. Hybrid names are indicated by an x: Lemon is *Citrus x limon*, orange is *Citrus x sinensis*, etc. The wild, "OG" citrus varieties include tangerine (*Citrus reticulata*), pomelo (*Citrus maxima*), and citron (*Citrus medica*). (Want to go down a fun, fruity internet rabbit hole? Look up "fingered citron," also known as the Buddha's hand lemon.)

Other name: Tolerable Floridians

Who it's good for: People who want to avoid scurvy and get free houseplants; ambitious and patient plant owners with access to bright sunlight

Appearance: Citrus trees are broadleaf evergreens that can reach up to 20 feet (6 m) outdoors. New leaves are red when they emerge and turn dark, glossy green with pale green undersides. Blossoms have four or five white petals and a beautiful fragrance. Be careful: Roses aren't the only garden plant that can stealthily stab your hands. Many citrus species, including lemons, have thorns.

Where you know it from: Aggressive marketing campaigns by the Florida Tourism Board; the section of the grocery store we blow past on the way to get beer and cereal

Where it's actually from: Wild citrus species are from tropical Asia, while many popular varieties were bred and developed from Asia to the Mediterranean.

HOW NOT TO KILL IT

🪴 **Space, pot, and soil requirements:** With citrus trees, it makes a difference to splurge on terra-cotta or porous clay pots. They love the airflow. Little homegrown trees should be repotted every two to three years. If you spring for a big, mature tree from a nursery or garden center, it is more likely to bear fruit if you repot it every spring. No matter what, remember: *Drainage is everything.*

Homegrown citrus starts off well in regular seedling mixes and potting soil, but thrives with citrus fertilizer. You can also crush up clean, dry eggshells and add them to the soil if you're unwilling to shell out (yes, I went there) for fancy fertilizer.

Cooler winter temperatures encourage citrus trees to flower. If your citrus tree flowers indoors, consider pollinating it by hand with a tiny, clean paintbrush. (At least your lemon tree is getting some action.)

≈ **Water requirements:** Citrus likes to be well watered, but follow the refill rule. In the winter, slow down on the water and stop applying fertilizer.

🌾 **Light requirements:** Keep these plants next to a window (south-facing, if your home permits). They like full sun and thrive with four or more hours of direct sunlight. The lower-maintenance Meyer lemon tolerates partial shade.

☠ **Toxicity:** Toxic to cats and dogs

Other tips and facts: It's possible to grow lemons, oranges, kumquats, grapefruits, and other citrus varieties from seed as houseplants. Use fresh seeds and rinse them well to remove the sugary gel that sticks to the seed coat. If you skip this step, the seeds are less likely to germinate, and they may develop fungus if they do. Keep covered, sown seeds in a warm place, such as the top of your refrigerator (if safe from cats). Once they sprout, in three to six weeks, move them to an area where they can get as much bright light as possible.

Citrus has some bizarre reproductive habits. Don't be surprised to find multiple seedlings growing out of each seed. The biggest, strongest seedling (the healthiest houseplant) is the result of pollination, while the smaller seedlings are vegetatively produced (apomictic) offspring. These smaller plants are genetic clones of the parent plant. (If you worry about turning into one of your parents in middle age, imagine how bad these creatures have it.)

Unlike avocado trees, your homegrown citrus may actually produce fruit in your lifetime. Key lime trees produce fruit in as little as four years, while other citrus varieties take about six to seven. If the first year's fruits are funky or sour, give the tree a pass, or settle for making marmalade. The next season's fruits are likely to be better. If you want to buy a mature citrus that will produce fruit, consider a Meyer lemon. The trees themselves are smaller than other varieties, and the lemons have a sweeter flavor and thinner peel than most grocery store lemons. Most importantly, these are some of the easiest citrus trees to keep alive.

Corn Plant and Dragon Tree

(Dracaena fragrans and Dracaena marginata)

Common names: Corn plant and dragon tree

Botanical names: *Dracaena fragrans* and *Dracaena marginata*. The genus name comes from *Drakaina*, Greek for a female dragon. *Fragrans* refers to the corn plant's fragrant flowers and *marginata* refers to the dragon tree's distinctive leaf margins.

Other names: Fragrant dracaena, Madagascar dragon tree, song of India

Who it's good for: People who like the idea of corn but want to be nowhere near a farm; *Game of Thrones* fans

Appearance: Corn plant grows on vertical, unbranched stems. Most houseplant specimens have thick, bluntly cut stems with rosettes of bright green, strappy leaves emerging from the sides. Unfortunately, the whimsical chains of fragrant, puffball flowers for which the species is named rarely appear on houseplants. Dragon tree has thin, gray, upright stems that end in tufts of slender, spiky leaves up to 2 feet (60 cm) long and a 1/2 inch (1 cm) wide. The leaves are green with a distinctive red edge. As the lower leaves fall off, they leave behind a diamond-shaped pattern on the stem. In the wild, both trees can reach up to 20 feet (6 m) in height, but houseplants max out at 6 feet (2 m) and can be pruned shorter.

Where you know it from: If you ever picked at the wax cap over a plant's cut stem in the orthodontist's waiting room as a kid, there's a 99 percent chance that was a corn plant.

Where it's actually from: Corn plant is native to tropical Africa. (Corn plant is not related to actual corn, *Zea mays*, which is native to southern Mexico.) Dragon tree is native to the islands of Madagascar and Mauritius.

HOW NOT TO KILL IT

🪴 **Space, pot, and soil requirements:** If your plant starts to lift out of its container or sends roots out through the drainage holes, it's time to repot it. Regrettably, changes in temperature, drafts, and a lack of drainage can cause sudden, massive leaf loss, a drawback these plants share with my nemesis, the trendy and capricious fiddle leaf fig (*Ficus* *lyrata*, not profiled). Once your corn plant or dragon tree has a comfortable spot in your home, try not to move it.

≈ **Water requirements:** Keep these plants' soil consistently damp in spring and summer, then allow the soil to dry out slightly between waterings in the fall and winter. Drain off the excess water that collects in the saucer or cachepot. If your plant is unhappy with the amount of water it's getting, it will warn you with brown leaves. If you're watering well and still seeing discolored leaves, it may be due to fluoride in the tap water. Avoid using cold water on these plants.

☀ **Light requirements:** These plants like bright, indirect light. While they tolerate low light, too little light will cause the leaves to lose their color. Direct sun can cause the leaves to develop dry streaks and patches, kind of like those shards of sunburn that give away anyone who still doesn't understand that spray-on sunscreen needs to be rubbed in.

☠ **Toxicity:** Toxic if eaten (saponins)

> **Other tips and facts:** If your corn plant or dragon tree grows too tall, you can propagate it the way King Solomon facetiously suggested dividing a baby: Cut it in half. Just hack off the top of a stem and root it as a new plant. New growth will quickly emerge on the old stem just below the cut. Pruned stems may grow two or more branches.

Donkey Tail
(Sedum morganianum)

Common name: Donkey tail

Botanical name: *Sedum morganianum*

Other name: Burro's tail

Who it's good for: People who can resist the urge to touch it. So, probably no one.

Appearance: This delicate, sensitive succulent grows heavy stems up to 4 feet (1.3 m) long that are packed with spirals of overlapping, blue-green leaves that look like pointy jelly beans. The leaves have a silvery, powdery coating called a “bloom” that rubs off when touched. Happy plants may send out pink or red flower clusters at the ends of the stems in the summer.

Where you know it from: It’s the most popular fake plant at T.J. Maxx.

Where it’s actually from: Honduras and southern Mexico

HOW NOT TO KILL IT

Space, pot, and soil requirements: Little specimens with short, upright stems do well in a variety of pots, but mature donkey tail plants like raised or hanging pots from which their stems can hang down. This plant loves to be left alone and rarely needs repotting. It can still thrive when pot-bound. If your donkey tail has completely filled its container, repot it in the spring.

≈ **Water requirements:** Donkey tail follows the refill rule. Let the soil dry out almost completely between waterings. If the leaves stay plump, your plant is getting enough water. If they start to look like old grapes from the back of the fridge, give it more. You may not need to water your donkey tail more than once a month.

Light requirements: Give your donkey tail bright light. It loves full sun. If it’s too dark, the stems will grow longer, leaving more space between the leaves. If it’s too bright, the leaves will turn yellow.

Toxicity: Nontoxic

Other tips and facts: Don't touch or handle this plant more than necessary. The bloom will wipe away in streaks and the delicate leaves are prone to breaking off. Mercifully, they're not a threat to foraging pets. However, if you want more of this magical jelly bean plant, you're in luck. Leaves that break off may grow roots to become teeny new specimens. Donkey tail is also easy to propagate through cuttings or division.

If you treat your donkey tail well, it could live for decades.

Elephant Ears and Taro

(Alocasia spp. and Colocasia esculenta)

Common names:
Elephant ears and taro

Botanical names: There are
multiple species of *Alocasia* and

Colocasia. These names come
from the Greek word *kolokasia,*
which refers to the edible roots
of the lotus plant (*Nelumbo
nucifera*). *Esculenta* is Latin for

"edible" and a convenient code word for weed brownies.

Other names: Taro is also known as kalo, dasheen, cocoyam, ubi keladi, and eddoe.

Who it's good for: Homesick Hawaiians; enthusiastic overwaterers; fans of *My Neighbor Totoro* who feel a sense of magic and nostalgia from extra-large foliage

Appearance: Elephant ears and taro have clusters of long, succulent stems that emerge from tuberous rhizomes (thick, fleshy roots). The leaves are heart shaped or arrowhead shaped and range in color from lime green to black, sometimes with sharply contrasting leaf veins. (Elephant ear leaves point upward; taro leaves point downward.) The leaves can reach 8 to 36 inches (20 to 91 cm) and mature plants can reach between 2 and 6 feet (0.6 and 2 m) in height.

A common elephant ear is the *Alocasia* x *amazonica* hybrid. It has leathery, dark green leaves with wavy edges and silvery, pastel-green leaf veins. While taro is more common as a landscape plant, it can be grown indoors with enough space. Mature specimens can reach 6 feet (2 m) in height and spread. For goth/emo taro, try the 'Black Magic' and 'Black Coral' varieties.

Where you know it from: Taro is the state plant of Hawai'i and a common vegetable across tropical Asia and the Pacific Islands.

Where it's actually from: Tropical Southeast Asia. *Alocasia* x *amazonica* is a trade name, not a scientific one. These plants are from Asia, not South America. It's possible that 'Amazonica' refers to Amazon Nursery in Miami, Florida, where these plants were hybridized in the 1950s. Ask Alexa.

HOW NOT TO KILL IT

⊟ **Space, pot, and soil requirements:** Use a rich, dark potting soil. When picking a container, go for drainage and stability. With such giant leaves, bigger specimens risk tipping over. Use a heavy clay container or add some rocks to the bottom of a regular pot, which also helps drainage. Keeping these plants in smaller pots can prevent them from reaching their full size if space is an issue.

≈ **Water requirements:** Keep these plants moist, but not drowning, and do not let the soil dry out between waterings. If your home is very dry, mist these plants with a spray bottle. They'll be happier than a golden retriever getting to drink from the garden hose.

🌿 **Light requirements:** Elephant ears and taro prefer indirect light and partial shade. In bright, direct sun, they can turn pale or sunburn. Light green varieties can tolerate brighter light than darker varieties.

☠ **Toxicity:** Toxic if eaten (fatal to pets). Only fully cooked taro roots are safe to eat. Handle with gloves, as sap can irritate and burn skin.

Other tips and facts: Elephant ears and taro are easy to propagate by division. A rhizome just needs one leaf on it to get started as a new plant. Mealybugs and scale love their soft leaves. If your plants are afflicted, prune off affected foliage rather than scraping the bugs off.

If you're interested in eating taro, look for it at farmers' markets and Asian markets. Your houseplant won't make a tasty meal, especially if you're growing a variety developed for its looks.

Taro is a revered plant with a rich history. It's been cultivated as a crop for more than six thousand years and all parts of the plant are used in some type of cuisine: The tubers are combined with coconut to make poi in Hawai'i and Polynesia, and the leaves and petioles (leaf stems) are used as vegetables in Malaysia, Myanmar, Nepal, and China. Soviet cosmonauts supposedly ate rehydrated taro packets in space, because taro has more vitamin A, vitamin C, calcium, and protein than potatoes. It's a space potato, just like me. (See Ponytail Palm, page 63.)

Holiday Cacti

(Schlumbergera spp.)

Common names: Easter cactus, Thanksgiving cactus, Christmas cactus. These cacti are named for the approximate time of year that they flower.

Botanical names: *Schlumbergera gaertneri* (Easter cactus), *Schlumbergera truncata* (Thanksgiving cactus), *Schlumbergera* x *buckleyi* or *Schlumbergera bridgesii* (Christmas cactus). There's disagreement over whether the genus is named for the French Frédéric Schlumberger or the Belgian Frederick Schlumberger, both nineteenth-century horticulturists. I think it's the French guy, who preferred tending to his cactus collection over continuing the family textile business.

Other name: Crab cactus

Who it's good for: Green succulent lovers who appreciate this plant's year-round Medusa vibe; ambitious blossom lovers with the patience, latitude, and regular sleep schedule to make it flower

Appearance: Holiday cacti grow in a symmetrical spray of fleshy branches made of flattened segments called phylloclades. Flowers bloom from the ends of the branches and can last up to eight weeks. Holiday cacti flower in a variety of colors, including white, lavender, pink, peach, orange, and dark red.

The branch segments' shapes help differentiate between the species. Easter cactus's segments are oval shaped. Thanksgiving cactus has crab-like stem segments with two to four pointy "teeth" along the sides. Christmas cactus has smoother, teardrop-shaped stem segments.

Where you know it from: This was a popular midcentury houseplant. A giant Christmas cactus dominated the plant stand on my grandmother's West Georgia patio for decades, where it grew strong on secondhand smoke and public broadcasting.

Where it's actually from: Unexpectedly, these true cacti are from the shady, humid rainforests of Brazil, where they grow as epiphytes on trees.

HOW NOT TO KILL IT

🪴 **Space, pot, and soil requirements:** Holiday cacti do best in a hanging container or on a plant stand. These plants need a super-light soil mix that allows maximum drainage and airflow. Using a terra-cotta or unglazed clay pot supports both. These cacti don't mind being cozy.

They're still comfortable when pot-bound. Most holiday cacti only need to be repotted every three years or so.

≈ **Water requirements:** Follow the refill rule and err on the side of dryness. To encourage flowers, increase watering in the month or two before your cactus's holiday bloom time so that the soil stays evenly moist, without getting heavy or waterlogged.

🌾 **Light requirements:** To keep your holiday cactus alive, give it filtered light or partial shade. Full sun is great during fall and winter, but the intensity of full summer sun can bleach the phylloclades and turn them yellow. For flowering, light is more complicated. Thanksgiving and Christmas cacti are "short-day plants" that need long nights and short days (eight to ten hours of light) to bloom, whereas Easter cacti are the opposite: They need short nights and long days to bloom. If the natural day length in your area is sufficient, simply leave your holiday cactus in a room with a window and don't turn any lights on.

☠ **Toxicity:** Nontoxic to pets

> **Other tips and facts:** If all three holiday cacti are available for sale, the Thanksgiving and Christmas cacti are slightly easier to care for. Easter cacti are more prone to dropping branch segments if over- or underwatered.
>
> Put your holiday cactus in your will and testament along with your jade plant (whether as assets or beneficiaries depends on how posthumously petty you want to be). These plants can survive for more than a hundred years.

Lady Palm
(*Rhapis excelsa*)

Common name: Lady palm

Botanical name: *Rhapis excelsa*. The genus name comes from *rhapis*, Greek for needle. The Latin species name *excelsa* refers to the plant's height (a questionable moniker because this is not the tallest of the *Rhapis* palms).

Other name: Bamboo palm

Who it's good for: Indulgent plant owners ready for a glamorous but sensitive botanical roommate. If this plant were human, it'd make mean cocktails and own a fainting couch.

Appearance: Lady palms grow in clusters of stems covered with dark brown fiber that looks like woven burlap (say "homespun tweed" to protect their feelings). Fan-shaped leaves emerge from the tops and sides of the stems. Each leaf is deeply divided into five to eight narrow, finger-like segments with blunt tips, like a botanical hand turkey. Houseplants tend to max out at 6 feet (2 m). Lady palms are dioecious, meaning that male and female flowers develop on separate plants (the same goes for date palms, whereas coconut palms are monoecious and have "all the parts" on one tree). Though it's unlikely, indoor lady palms may put forth panicles (chandelier-like clusters) of tiny yellow flowers in the spring.

Lady palm is the only palm species available in both a green form and a variegated form with cream-colored streaks. The variegated cultivars are rare and grow more slowly.

Where you know it from: The bathrooms at an upscale Asian fusion restaurant, next to a fountain and a tiny Buddha statue

Where it's actually from: Southeastern China and Vietnam

HOW NOT TO KILL IT

🏺 **Space, pot, and soil requirements:** Like kentia palms, lady palms are OK with being root-bound and can comfortably stay in the same pot for several years. When it's time, repot this palm in spring or early summer and be careful not to damage the fragile roots. Use an extra-rich potting soil such as African violet mix: These prissy palms have expensive taste. Unlike many houseplants, lady palms tolerate drafts and do well near doors, where they absorb gossip.

≈ **Water requirements:** Follow the refill rule with this palm and water it when the soil is dry to the touch. Give it a thorough drench, then drain off any excess water that collects in the saucer or cachepot. Browning leaves can indicate dry soil or dry air. If you're watering well and still seeing brown, try misting the palm with a spray bottle once a week.

🌿 **Light requirements:** Lady palms like indirect light and can tolerate deep shade (absence of light, not thinly veiled criticism). Try to situate your lady palm close to a window, but out of direct sun, which can scorch and burn the leaves.

☠ **Toxicity:** Nontoxic to pets

Other tips and facts: Many palm species can only be propagated by seed, but clustering palms like this one can be divided up when repotting in spring or early summer. Be gentle, go slowly, leave as many roots intact as possible, and expect some jealousy between the new rivals.

Scale and mealybugs are major pests and can be hard to detect among the dark fibers covering the stems and leaf bases. If your palm is afflicted, take it on a brief trip outside when temperatures are above 50°F (10°C). Rainfall and predators can make a major dent in the infestation. Frame it as a "natural spa treatment" to talk the palm into it.

Parlor Palm

(Chamaedorea elegans)

Common name: Parlor palm

Botanical name:
Chamaedorea elegans

Other names: Neanthe bella palm, bamboo palm, dwarf palm, good luck palm

Who it's good for: People with pets who still have seasonal affective disorder; people who like the value of getting lots of little palms for the price of one

Appearance: Parlor palms are small, usually with a single trunk. Seedlings are often planted and sold in groups of five to thirty. In containers, they can reach about 4 feet (1.3 m). Their dense, arching leaves have twelve or more narrow leaflets. With enough light, even small parlor palms put out spirals of yellow flowers in the spring. The fruit looks like small black olives (DO NOT EAT).

Where you know it from: This is the "Palm Sunday" palm, also used in floral arrangements.

Where it's actually from: The rainforests of Guatemala and Mexico

HOW NOT TO KILL IT

⛝ **Space, pot, and soil requirements:** Parlor palms are happy competing with one another in their tight little groves. They tolerate crowded roots and should only be repotted when necessary. Every other year is usually enough. Keep these palms away from drafty areas like doors, vents, and poorly insulated windows.

≈ **Water requirements:** Parlor palms like to be consistently damp, but don't overdo it. They can tolerate drought, but overwatering will turn them to yellow slime. Scale back further in the winter. Give these palms a mist from time to time if they're in a heated room. If the leaves start to curl or look crispy, check both the soil moisture and the humidity.

🌿 **Light requirements:** These plants were popular in Victorian English households for a reason: They can survive the darkness and the dankness. Keep them away from full sun and dry air. Bright, indirect light, such as from an east- or north-facing window is ideal.

☠ Toxicity: Nontoxic

Other tips and facts: Prepare psychologically. If you've purchased a cluster of these small palms, expect some death, and know it's not your fault. Over time, the weaker palms will die off, leaving a batch of stronger houseplants that can survive for decades. It's like a slow-motion battle royale for tiny trees. You can also proactively divide the clustered palms into separate pots. Just be as gentle with the roots as possible.

Prayer Plants

(Calathea spp. and Maranta spp.)

Common name: Prayer plants

Botanical names: Examples include *Calathea lancifolia*

(rattlesnake plant), *Calathea zebrina* (zebra plant), *Calathea ornata* (beauty star), *Calathea veitchiana* (calathea medallion), and *Maranta leuconeura* (cathedral windows, rabbit tracks).

Other name: Peacock plants

Who it's good for: People who want colorful plants, but not flowers; people who overuse the "prayer hands" emoji; white people who like to explain the difference between "namaste" and "namaskar"; people who want a needy plant baby in addition to their needy fur babies

Appearance: Prayer plants are compact, ground-dwelling plants known for their wacky, surprising foliage and named for their tendency to open in light and close in darkness. Leaves range from short and round to long and pointy, with dark or colorful stripes, and many leaves have purple undersides. *C. lancifolia*, the rattlesnake plant, looks like it's been brushed with India ink. My personal favorite, *C. ornata* (the shamelessly named "beauty star"), has dark green oval leaves with pastel pink stripes that look like they were painted on with nail polish. Most prayer plants max out at about 12 inches (30 cm) in height. Indoor plants are unlikely to flower, but if they do, you'll see small blossoms in pink, white, or orange that look like stacked baskets.

Where you know it from: The landscaping in front of that Airbnb on Hawai'i you keep looking at online

Where it's actually from: All over tropical South America

HOW NOT TO KILL IT

🝊 **Space, pot, and soil requirements:** Drainage is big for prayer plants. If you repot one, add some pebbles or gravel to the bottom of the pot.

≈ **Water requirements:** These plants take exception to the refill rule.

They like to be evenly moist, and they like high humidity. If the soil is appropriately damp but the leaves still curl or crisp, mist the leaves with a spray bottle. Yellow leaves will show you if you're overwatering.

≈ **Light requirements:** Feel free to throw some shade at these plants, literally. They are happiest in indirect light. Most of these species will scorch or sunburn in full sun.

☠ **Toxicity:** Nontoxic

Other tips and facts: Pay attention to your prayer plants daily and watch for leaves that are getting crispy or wrinkly. Prune off discolored or dry leaves at the base. Fortunately, even a prayer plant that looks dead may send up healthy new leaves with the proper care. If you think you've killed it, prune it, water it, give it time, and sure, pray for it if you feel compelled.

Prayer plants are also easy to propagate by division. If you take a prayer plant out of its pot, you'll see round yellow or white root nodules that store water and nutrients. It's this storage capacity that enables the plant's resurrection from sunburn, dehydration, or neglect. Try to include a few root nodules and several leaves in each division.

Want a prayer plant relative with a teal, cream, and mauve 1980s-upholstery color scheme? Look for *Stromanthe thalia*.

Rubber Fig

(Ficus elastica)

Common name: Rubber fig

Botanical name: Ficus *elastica*. The genus name *Ficus* comes from the Latin word for "fig,"

and *elastica* refers to the sap that was used to make rubber in the early twentieth century. It has since been replaced by the commercially superior

Pará rubber tree (*Hevea brasiliensis*). Ficus elastica is now just grown for its looks.

Other name: Indian rubber plant

Who it's good for: People who want the beauty of a magnolia and can handle the demands of a fussy ficus (dusting, pruning, minor pest treatment)

Appearance: Rubber fig plants have dark, leathery, oval leaves that can grow up to 12 inches (30 cm) long. In the wild, these trees develop aerial roots and can reach heights of 100 feet (30 m). Your houseplant will likely be between 2 and 10 feet (0.6 and 3 m). Outdoor plants develop small, inedible figs (not toxic, just disgusting), but your houseplant is highly unlikely to flower or fruit.

Where you know it from: Viral images of living root bridges across rivers in Meghalaya, India. (You can show these to your plant if you want to shame it for not living up to its potential, but don't be surprised if it emails you the press release from your sister's National Science Foundation grant.)

Where it's actually from: South and Southeast Asia, from the Himalayas to the islands of Java and Sumatra

HOW NOT TO KILL IT

🏺 **Space, pot, and soil requirements:** The rubber fig isn't picky when it comes to potting soil, but it can't stand cold temperatures or drafts: It will drop leaves. Keep it away from doors or poorly insulated windows. If it's comfortable, leave it be. The fussier ficus species don't like to be moved.

≈ **Water requirements:** Give this tree regular water in the spring and summer, letting the soil dry slightly in between. Reduce watering in fall and winter. If you overwater your rubber fig, it will let you know by dropping *yellow* leaves, specifically. Drain off excess water that collects in the saucer or cachepot.

🌿 **Light requirements:** Rubber figs like bright, indirect light and can tolerate partial shade and low light. They're especially happy in east-facing windows.

☠ **Toxicity:** Toxic to pets. Wear gloves to prune and repot.

> **Other tips and facts:** Rubber figs' thick, smooth leaves are appealing to spider mites, scale, and especially mealybugs. If you see them, try wiping them off with a damp cloth before they take over.
>
> These trees can grow tall. Prune your rubber fig to keep it small and shrubby or leave it alone for a tall tree that can fill a room. Keep in mind that ficus trees' latex sap can irritate skin, so handle your rubber fig with gloves.

Sago Palm

(Cycas revoluta)

Common name: Sago palm

Botanical name: *Cycas revoluta*. *Cyca* comes from *kykas* or *koikas*, Greek words for a type of palm tree. Although they look like palms, cycads are more closely related to gingko trees.

Other names: Japanese sago palm, king sago palm. Sago is a type of edible starch harvested from these plants, used primarily in New Guinea. Most commercial sago comes from a true palm, *Metroxylon sagu*.

Who it's good for: People who want a "dinosaur plant." The cycad family dates back over 200 million years. They have barely evolved. If it ain't broke, don't fix it.

Appearance: Cycads look like giant, zany (inedible!) pineapples. Thick, dark, sharp, palm-like fronds emerge in a symmetrical whorl from a small, scruffy trunk. Houseplants reach 2 to 3 feet (60 to 91 cm) in height. Sago palms are dioecious, meaning that there are separate male and female plants. Not to be outdone by any aroids, male cycads put up comically phallic yellow pollen cones that are 12 to 18 inches (30 to 45 cm) tall. The female cones look like feathery orbs and produce large, fleshy, bright-red seeds the size of dates. Your indoor houseplants will be sexually inhibited, and you may never know what you've got, so don't plan a gender reveal party for your plant.

Where you know it from: Prehistoric dioramas at natural history museums. Sago palms are also popular landscape plants in South Carolina, Georgia, Florida, and California.

Where it's actually from: Southern China and southern Japan (Kyushu and the Ryukyu Islands)

HOW NOT TO KILL IT

⊟ **Space, pot, and soil requirements:** These plants grow so slowly, you won't need to repot them often, possibly not for years. They tolerate being root-bound and are comfortable in a tight, cozy pot. If you do repot a sago palm, use a sandy succulent mix and wear thick gloves to protect your hands. Place your sago palm away from high-traffic areas, because the sharp leaves can scratch and irritate skin.

≈ **Water requirements:** Sago palms like a good, deep watering. Allow the soil surface to dry in between. Take special care to give sago palms plenty of water while they're developing their soft new leaves, otherwise the new growth will scorch or harden in a curled or crumpled shape.

🌾 **Light requirements:** Sago palms like filtered sun. They do well near windows with sheer curtains. Keep them out of direct sunlight: Too much sun can damage the foliage.

☠ **Toxicity:** Highly toxic if eaten. Handle with gloves.

Other tips and facts: Prune any dry, yellow leaves by cutting them off at the base. If you cut off all the leaves or apply a hefty dose of fertilizer, your sago palm will send up a fresh set of fronds.

Handle sago palms with care: They contain cycasin, a neurotoxin that can cause paralysis and a host of gastrointestinal hells. The bright red seeds contain the highest levels. Your houseplant is extremely unlikely to bear seeds, but you may see them on outdoor plants. Do not touch. Not scary enough? The root nodules contain cyanobacteria (blue-green algae) that help the plant fix nitrogen and are also neurotoxic. Always wear thick, waterproof gloves when repotting cycads.

Cycads are my favorite plants. Not only are they in no hurry to grow or produce anything, but they're also some of the most lucrative illegally traded plants in the world and a frequent target of theft in botanical gardens. Sago palms are not endangered, but many related species are nearing extinction in the wild. For a peek into this high-stakes conservation debacle, look up Operation Botany, a two-year undercover sting operation by THE most glamorous of federal agencies, the U.S. Fish and Wildlife Service.

Strangling Fig
(Ficus microcarpa)

Common name: Strangling fig

Botanical name: *Ficus microcarpa*. The 'Golden Gate' and 'Ginseng' cultivars are bonsai versions frequently sold as houseplants.

Other names: Curtain fig, laurel fig, small-fruited fig, glossy-leaved fig, Indian laurel, Chinese banyan, Malay banyan

Who it's good for: People who want to merge their interests in bonsai and erotic art with one cheeky plant. If you've seen photos online of a voluptuous little tree posing suggestively, it was probably this one.

Appearance: The strangling fig has dark, leathery, oval-shaped leaves and tiny, concave flowers that develop into figs only if pollinated by a single species of wasp, *Eupristina verticillata*. This tree can either grow as a shrub or a climber depending on the environment. In the wild, it germinates in the canopy, 80 feet (25 m) off the ground, where it can get some light and outcompete plants on the forest floor. Over time, the aerial roots grow down to the ground, creating a freestanding structure for the tree to stand on that eventually kills the plants underneath. In containers, strangling figs can reach 13 feet (4 m), but most houseplants are bonsais.

Where you know it from: Buckling, trip-hazard sidewalks in coastal California; vulgar plant memes

Where it's actually from: A wide swath of Asia and Oceania, including Sri Lanka, India, parts of southern China and Taiwan, Japan, northern Australia, New Caledonia, and other Pacific Islands

HOW NOT TO KILL IT

☐ **Space, pot, and soil requirements:** Strangling figs do best in a ceramic pot with big drainage holes. If your plant is a bonsai, prepare to repot it every two years. (Try using "I can't, I'm repotting my bonsai" as an excuse to cancel plans and feel yourself age forty years.)

≈ **Water requirements:** Keep the soil moist but well drained. These plants like consistent moisture. If your space is dry, mist these plants every once in a while to prevent leaf drop. At least strangling figs drop crispy confetti that a Roomba can handle, unlike my nemesis, the trendy and capricious fiddle leaf fig (*Ficus lyrata*, not profiled), which drops leaves the size of dinner plates.

🌾 **Light requirements:** Give this plant a spot near a south-facing window. It likes filtered sunlight to full sun. Light will affect the size of the leaves. Indoor bonsai ficus in lower light tend to produce larger leaves, whereas bonsai ficus outdoors or in the brightest light will produce smaller leaves.

☠ **Toxicity:** Toxic if eaten. Wear gloves when pruning.

Other tips and facts: Prune this little ficus to maintain its shape and wear gloves when you do: Ficus sap is irritating. Ficus are heavy feeders, so give this tree fertilizer every two weeks in the spring and summer.

This species' reliance on a single wasp for pollination made it a great landscape plant, in theory. It tolerates salt, drought, and high winds, so it's well suited for coastal areas. Without their pollinators, these trees stayed put. In the 1990s, however, the *E. verticillata* wasp made its way into Southern California, and the ensuing fig-fest turned this tree into an invasive species. It is now "widely known to escape from cultivation."

String of Pearls

(Curio rowleyanus)

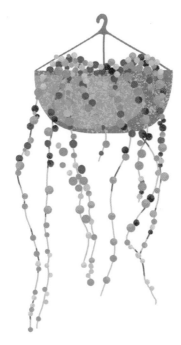

Common name: String of pearls

Botanical names: *Curio rowleyanus* or *Senecio rowleyanus*. The genus name *Senecio* comes from *senex*, Latin for "old man," and refers to

the seeds' white pappus (fluffy hair, similar to a dandelion's). The species is named after the late Gordon Douglas Rowley, a British botanist who named his house "Cactusville" and published his last botanical book at the age of ninety-five.

Other names: String of beads, pearl plant

Who it's good for: Committed preppy aesthetes who mourned the J.Crew bankruptcy and give their houseplants double-barreled names; people who can keep this aloof plant princess away from children and animals

Appearance: String of pearls develops long, trailing stems up to 3 feet (1 m) in length. In the wild, these stems take root where nodes touch the ground and form dense mats of groundcover. The "pearls" are alternating, nearly spherical leaves about ¼ inch (6 mm) in diameter that store water. Each leaf has a tiny, pointed tip at the end and a band of darker, translucent tissue that supports photosynthesis by allowing extra light into the leaf.

Well-bred string of pearls is an aster, in the same family as daisies and sunflowers. In the summer, this plant develops compound flowers that look like the coronavirus: round clusters of tiny white blossoms with red stamens sticking out.

Where you know it from: You guessed it: It's another high-touch surface at the botanical garden, with what looks like a pile of mashed peas right underneath the "please do not touch" sign.

Where it's actually from: The Eastern Cape of South Africa

HOW NOT TO KILL IT

⬱ **Space, pot, and soil requirements:** String of pearls thrives and looks best in a hanging basket or a container on a plant stand. Either of these setups allows the trailing stems to hang down comfortably. Use a shallow container for this shallow plant. Unglazed clay that allows for greater airflow is ideal. Drainage is also crucial for string of pearls, so use a sandy succulent mix or mix regular potting soil one-to-one with sand or pea gravel. String of pearls can be repotted every spring.

≈ Water requirements: Allow this plant to dry out between watering. String of pearls tolerates some neglect when it comes to watering and can handle dry spells. Poorly drained, stodgy soils are a bigger threat. If the pearls begin to shrivel, give this plant a drink.

≋ Light requirements: This plant does not like to be out on display as much as its name would suggest. String of pearls likes partial shade. In the wild, it grows underneath other plants and between rocks, out of the full sun.

☠ Toxicity: Toxic if eaten. The sap can cause an irritating skin rash.

Other tips and facts: Even a well-cared-for string of pearls will begin to die back after a few years, but you can withhold that information from smug "plant parents" who need to be taken down a peg. At that point, take stem cuttings or start fresh. If you haven't repotted your string of pearls into fresh soil within one or two years, give it a light fertilizer feed in the spring.

Forego this plant if you have a toddler. The pearls are a pediatrician's nightmare: toxic and a choking hazard. Ingestion can cause diarrhea and vomiting in mammals, and I don't want your child to develop a lifelong phobia of green grapes.

Master Gardener Houseplant

Monstera

(Monstera deliciosa)

Common names: Monstera, Swiss cheese plant

Botanical name: *Monstera deliciosa*, the delicious monster. The 'Albo Variegata' and 'Variegata' cultivars are popular.

Other names: Hurricane plant, Mexican breadfruit, split-leaf philodendron, windowleaf, tarovine

Who it's good for: Skilled gardeners who received this book as a thoughtless or last-minute gift (once you're known as a "plant person," there's just no stopping it); people with plenty of space to display and repot a botanical beast

Appearance: Monsteras are lianas, a type of vine that grows on other plants in the wild. Young monsteras have small, heart-shaped, solid leaves that climb up trees or posts in an overlapping shingle pattern. Once mature, monsteras produce the giant, glossy, heart-shaped leaves for which they're famous (up to 18 inches [45 cm]), with holes called "fenestrations" that allow heavy winds to blow through without damage. Wild monsteras can reach 70 feet (21 m) and grow aerial roots that reach out to attach to tree trunks and branches. If they touch the soil, they take root. Your monstera houseplant will likely max out at 6 to 8 feet (2 to 2.5 m).

Where you know it from: Every Instagram post from 2013 to 2018. If you wore shutter shades and orange skinny jeans to Lollapalooza in 2008, you wore a monstera print shirt in 2015.

Where it's actually from: Rainforests of southern Mexico, Guatemala, Costa Rica, and Panama

HOW NOT TO KILL IT

⛁ **Space, pot, and soil requirements:** Young monsteras in their "shingle phase" need warm temperatures and high humidity. Mature monsteras can tolerate a wider range of conditions (unlike my nemesis, the trendy and capricious fiddle leaf fig—*Ficus lyrata*, not profiled). Be sure to provide a textured, vertical structure for this plant, such as a post covered with tree bark or moss. Monsteras grow quickly and need to be repotted often to support their roots. Without a trellis or a post to climb, monsteras will creep horizontally across your floor. Once a plant is comfortably attached to its support, it will grow much larger leaves.

If your monstera is growing aerial roots, give them a little help. Short ones near the top of the plant can be guided to the support post. Roots lower down can be tucked into the soil to help the plant take up more nutrients. You can also just prune them off if you need to remind it who's boss.

≈ **Water requirements:** Water monsteras deeply and heavily, but allow the soil to dry slightly in between. Be sure to water and/or spray the aerial roots attached to the support post as well. If a monstera gets too much water, it will "sweat," showing tiny beads of moisture on the leaves. If the air around the plant gets too dry, its leaves will turn brown.

☀ **Light requirements:** In order to mimic the even light these plants get in the rainforest, try to keep your monstera in bright, indirect light for most of the year. If possible, move your plant into direct sunlight in the winter. (A cachepot with wheels is helpful.) Mature monsteras grow well under artificial light, but they don't develop as many leaf holes in lower light. Contrarian baby monsteras grow toward the dark instead of the light. In the wild, seedlings perceive dark areas as indicators that a big tree is nearby for them to climb. If you're starting a baby, place its climbing post on the side of the container away from the window until the plant has begun to climb.

☠ Toxicity: Toxic if eaten (except for fully ripe fruit)

Other tips and facts: Happy monsteras are rapid growers that need regular pruning to prevent them from taking over your home. (Even if aerial roots grow to reach the thermostat, don't expect this monster to contribute to any utility bills.) Cut the stem back and pull some shallow roots as needed to keep the plant at a manageable size.

While you'll probably never see a flower on your houseplant, mature, outdoor monsteras produce flowers that look like a cross between a corncob and a cucumber. An 8- to 12-inch (20 to 30 cm) spadix develops over a year into a fruit that tastes like banana and pineapple. Definitely try one if you see it at a farmers' market, but don't expect your houseplant to produce any.

Glossary

Acid-loving plants: Plants that thrive in soil with a pH lower than 7. Common examples include disappointingly nonpsychedelic azaleas, hydrangeas, and gardenias. Fertilizers for acid-loving plants often add nutrients that are unavailable when soil is too basic (high pH; not sipping Starbucks and shopping for Ugg boots) as well as generally lowering the soil pH with added minerals.

Apomictic: A product of apomixis, asexual reproduction without fertilization. Apomictic seeds and seedlings are genetically identical to their parent plants. This is convenient for fruit growers who want more of the same tree and mercifully unavailable to mammals as a reproductive strategy.

Aroid: Aroids, also known as arums, are members of the Araceae family. These soft, herby plants all have phallic flowers and contain calcium oxalates that make them inedible to humans and pets. In short, a charming plant family to some and "toxic little dicks" to others.

Axil: The inner angle between a branch or leaf stalk and the branch, stem, or trunk out of which it grows. Pests like mealybugs love to concentrate in the axils of leaves.

Bloom: A gray or white powdery coating on succulent plants that protects against sunburn, water loss, and insects. Succulents with bloom effectively dust for fingerprints: Bloom wipes off easily, leaving evidence of inappropriate plant touching.

Cachepot: Also known as an indoor container. A solid, outer plant pot that collects water that has run through an interior pot's drainage holes, keeping the floor underneath dry. Savior of many apartment security deposits.

Caudex (pl. caudices): The thick base or stem of a perennial plant. Plants like ponytail palm and desert rose (*Adenium* spp.) have charmingly chunky, vase-like caudices that have evolved to store water.

Contact dermatitis: Itchy, inflamed skin resulting from exposure to an irritant such as plant sap. Wearing gloves to prune and repot houseplants is a wise first line of defense.

Epiphyte: A plant that grows on other plants but is not parasitic. Examples include bromeliads and ferns that grow on trees but do not extract any nutrients from their hosts or cause them any harm. Still living at home but contributing to household expenses? You're not a parasite, you're an epiphyte!

Extension: Programs and services facilitated by land-grant universities that offer education, training, and support on agriculture and horticulture topics to the public, free of charge. Look up what's available in your area. Extension programs offer help and information to everyone from industrial farmers to total houseplant newbies.

Honeydew: A clear, sticky, sugary fluid excreted by insects such as aphids, scale, and mealybugs. Note that this is not just dripping plant sap: It's sap that has gone *all the way through* the bugs. Honeydew can draw ants and lead to sooty mold on foliage.

Horticultural soap and oil: Petroleum- or vegetable-derived products used to remove mold and fungus and to treat insect infestations by dissolving the bugs' waxy coating. Usually mixed with water and applied as a spray.

Iron chlorosis: Iron deficiency in plants that leads to a yellowing between leaf veins. Fertilizer for acid-loving plants or a chelated iron spray can help treat this "houseplant anemia."

Leaflet: A leaf-like segment of a compound leaf. For example, many palm fronds are made up of ribbon-like, parallel leaflets. I deliberately misuse this term to baby-talk cute, tiny foliage.

Leggy: Stretched out and reaching for light. Plants in conditions that are too dark develop leggy growth. A great look for '90s high-fashion models, but an unfortunate one for houseplants.

Liana: What Tarzan swings from: a woody vine rooted in the soil that climbs trees and other plants to reach brighter sunlight throughout the tree canopy. Most lianas are found in tropical rainforests. A temperate exception is clematis, a purple-flowered climber that takes over trellises and fences.

Mesic: Growing in moderate moisture, as opposed to xeric plants, which grow in dry conditions.

Node: An area on a stem where buds are located, often where leaves, branches, and flowers emerge. Try to include several nodes when taking a cutting.

N-P-K: Nitrogen, phosphorus, and potassium, the three main nutrients in commercial fertilizers. Nitrogen supports foliage growth, phosphorus supports roots and flowers, and potassium helps plants tolerate stress. Fertilizer labels indicate the guaranteed percentages of these three nutrients available in the product.

Offset: Also known as a "pup" or a basal offset, a small, complete plant that emerges from the base of the parent plant, often after the parent plant has flowered. Many succulents, air plants, and bromeliads reproduce vegetatively

through offsets in addition to sexually reproducing with flowers. Most offsets can be removed from the parent plant and potted up as new plants.

Overpotting: Repotting a plant into a pot that's too large. Overpotted plants suffer similarly to overwatered plants. As a best practice, increase a plant's pot one size at a time.

Oxalate: A salt or ester of oxalic acid. Aroid plants contain high concentrations of calcium oxalate, making them toxic to humans and pets.

Panicle: A compound flower cluster with many branches. Panicles often appear fluffy and/or chandelier-like.

Pappus: Tufts of hair on seeds that help them disperse via the wind. Dandelion fluff is the most common example.

Petiole: The stalk that connects a leaf to a stem. A device to remember this term: Who arbitrarily picks leaves off of innocent plants? A petty ol' bastard.

Phylloclade: A modified branch or branch segment that

photosynthesizes like a leaf (e.g., the fleshy branches of holiday cacti).

Powdery mildew: A common fungus that shows up as powdery gray or white spots on leaves. Spores are everywhere naturally, but poor air circulation allows them to grow into a problem. Check plants regularly and prune off affected foliage.

Pseudostem: Overlapping or rolled-up leaves that give the appearance of a stem. Banana, ginger, and turmeric leaves all emerge as pseudostems.

Pup: Another, cuter term for an offset. A small, complete plant that emerges at the base of the parent plant.

Pyrethrin: A class of organic pesticide derived from chrysanthemum flowers. Pyrethrin compounds break down quickly and have low toxicity for humans and pets, but they are not completely harmless. Always follow product instructions and use as a last resort when other pest control methods have failed.

Rhizome: A thick, fleshy, modified underground stem that stores nutrients. Unlike tubers, which grow in any direction, rhizomes grow horizontally, sending roots downward and new shoots upward. Ginger and turmeric grow from rhizomes.

Scurf: Raised, light-colored, elongated, waxy spots that occur naturally on the new leaves of some palm species. Scurf can easily be mistaken for scale infestation. Also my preferred term for an ugly scarf.

Seed leaves: Also known as cotyledons, the first leaves to emerge on a newly sprouted seedling. These leaves are actually a part of the embryo. They last for a short time and provide food to the growing seedling, but do not photosynthesize and may not resemble the mature leaves of the plant.

Seed-starting mix: Also known as seedling mix, a fine, lightweight, well-drained mixture with little nutrition that enables seeds to germinate easily. Potting mixes are heavier, denser, and contain nutrients that mature plants need. Seeds come with their own store of food.

Short-day plant: A plant that needs an uninterrupted period of short days (less than twelve hours of sunlight) in order to flower. Chrysanthemums, poinsettias, and holiday cacti are all short-day plants. I lovingly refer to the late sleepers in my life as "short-day people."

Sooty mold: A black fungal infection caused by honeydew from an untreated insect infestation. Treat the pest problem causing the honeydew and try to wipe the mold off of the leaves using a paper towel and a mild soap solution.

Sorus (pl. sori): A small, round, spore-producing structure on the underside of a fern frond. Rhymes with "porous."

Spadix: A fleshy, floral spike that looks like a baby corncob or a small phallus, surrounded by a modified leaf called a spathe. All aroid flowers consist of a spadix and spathe. Flamingo flower blossoms are a great example.

Spathe: A large, sheath-like, modified leaf that partially encloses a flower cluster. Spathes may be colorful and mistaken for petals.

Stolon: An aboveground plant stem that creeps horizontally and can put down new roots from its nodes. Spider plants and Boston ferns spread horizontally via stolons.

Sucker: A secondary shoot arising from a plant's roots, usually on a tree. Some suckers can be taken as cuttings for new plants (e.g., from cycads). Pruning suckers off of trees is recommended, as they literally suck energy and nutrients from the main stem.

Terrestrial: Growing in the ground, as opposed to epiphytes, which grow on other plants.

Trichome: A fine outgrowth or hair. On air plants, trichomes make up the silvery fuzz that allow them to absorb both water and nutrients from the atmosphere.

True leaves: A seedling's first mature leaves that resemble the adult plant's foliage. These emerge after the seed leaves and can photosynthesize.

Tuber: A thick underground part of a stem or rhizome that stores food reserves for the plant and sends forth new buds. Potatoes are true tubers; sweet potatoes are technically just swollen, starchy roots. Unleash that factoid if you desperately need to change the subject at Thanksgiving dinner.

Tubercle: Not a tiny tuber, but a small nodule or projection. On succulents like haworthias, tubercles are special pores that allow the leaves to expand without tearing. On many cacti species, tubercles are points from which spines emerge.

Umbel: A compound flower in which short flower stalks emerge from a central point and create a round, flattened flower cluster. Cilantro and parsley flower in umbels, as do dill, carrots, and fennel. Also the name of my failed online dating start-up for vegetable growers.

Variegated: Displaying a variation in foliage color, usually white or yellow spots or streaks, caused by a lack of chlorophyll in those areas. These splotchy specimens are highly sought after and can fetch high prices.

Xeric: Requiring a tiny amount of moisture or thriving in dry conditions.

Selected Bibliography

Akers, Adam, Jo Barton, Rachel Cossey, Patrick Gainsford, Murray Griffin, and Dominic Micklewright. "Visual Color Perception in Green Exercise: Positive Effects on Mood and Perceived Exertion." *Environmental Science & Technology* 46, no. 16 (August 2012): 8661–66. https://doi.org/10.1021/es301685g.

American Society for the Prevention of Cruelty to Animals. "Toxic and Non-toxic Plants List." Poisonous Plants, Animal Poison Control, ASPCA.org. Accessed July 21, 2022. https://www.aspca.org/pet-care/animal-poison-control/toxic-and-non-toxic-plants.

Barceloux, Donald G. *Medical Toxicology of Natural Substances: Foods, Fungi, Medicinal Herbs, Plants, and Venomous Animals*. Hoboken: John Wiley & Sons, 2008.

Beukeboom, Camiel J., Dion Langeveld, and Karin Tanja-Dijkstra. "Stress-Reducing Effects of Real and Artificial Nature in a Hospital Waiting Room." *The Journal of Alternative and Complementary Medicine* 18, no. 4 (April 2012): 329–33. https://doi.org/10.1089/acm.2011.0488.

Brown, Deborah L. "Cacti and Succulents." Yard and Garden, University of Minnesota Extension. Reviewed 2018. Accessed December 3, 2021. https://extension.umn.edu/houseplants/cacti-and-succulents.

Dong, Qianni. "Problems Common to Many Indoor Plants." Gardening Help, Missouri Botanical Garden. Accessed November 4, 2021. https://www.missouribotanicalgarden.org/gardens-gardening/your-garden/help-for-the-home-gardener/advice-tips-resources/visual-guides/problems-common-to-many-indoor-plants.aspx.

Dorn, Sheri, and Bodie V. Pennisi. "Starting Plants from Seed for the Home Gardener." Bulletin 1432. University of Georgia Extension. Reviewed February 2018. Accessed December 3, 2021. https://secure.caes.uga.edu/extension/publications/files/pdf/B%201432_3.PDF.

Erler, Emma. "Fertilizing Houseplants." Blog, University of New Hampshire Extension. March 8, 2018. Accessed November 1, 2021. https://extension.unh.edu/blog/2018/03/fertilizing-houseplants.

Gowdy, Mary Ann. "Home Propagation of Houseplants." Lawn and Garden, University of Missouri Extension. Reviewed February 2012. Accessed November 4, 2021. https://extension.missouri.edu/media/wysiwyg/Extensiondata/Pub/pdf/agguides/hort/g06560.pdf.

Grinde, Bjørn, and Grete Grindal Patil. "Biophilia: Does Visual Contact with Nature Impact on Health and Well-Being?" *International Journal of Environmental Research and Public Health* 6, no. 9 (August 2009): 2332–43. https://dx.doi.org/10.3390%2Fijerph6092332.

Hahn, Jeff, and Julie Weisenhorn. "Managing Insects on Indoor Plants." Household Insects, University of Minnesota Extension. Reviewed 2020. Accessed November 1, 2021. https://extension.umn.edu/product-and-houseplant-pests/insects-indoor-plants.

Han, Ke-Tsung, and Li-Wen Ruan. "Effects of Indoor Plants on Air Quality: A Systematic Review." *Environmental Science and Pollution Research* 27 (May 2020): 16019–51. https://doi.org/10.1007/s11356-020-08174-9.

Home and Garden Information Center. "Indoor Plants." Clemson University Cooperative Extension. Accessed July 21, 2022. https://hgic.clemson.edu/category/indoor-plants/.

Kelley, Kathleen M., and Elsa S. Sánchez. "Growing Herbs Indoors." Penn State Extension. Updated October 22, 2007. Accessed December 4, 2021. https://extension.psu.edu/growing-herbs-indoors.

Klingaman, Gerald. "Plant of the Week." Cooperative Extension Service, University of Arkansas System Division of Agriculture. January 13, 2006. Accessed July 21, 2022. https://www.uaex.uada.edu/yard-garden/resource-library/plant-week/.

Ludwig, Ferdinand, Wilfrid Middleton, Friederike Gallenmüller, Patrick Rogers, and Thomas Speck. "Living Bridges Using Aerial Roots of *Ficus elastica*: An Interdisciplinary Perspective." *Scientific Reports* 9 (August 2019): 12226. https://www.nature.com/articles/s41598-019-48652-w.

Missouri Botanical Garden. "Plant Finder." Missouri Botanical Garden. Accessed July 21, 2022. http://www.missouribotanicalgarden.org/plantfinder/plantfindersearch.aspx.

National Gardening Association. "Plants Database." Garden.org. Accessed July 21, 2022. https://garden.org/plants/.

North Carolina State Extension. "North Carolina Extension Gardener Plant Toolbox." North Carolina Cooperative Extension. Accessed July 21, 2022. https://plants.ces.ncsu.edu/.

Pennisi, Bodie V. "Growing Indoor Plants with Success." Publications, University of Georgia Cooperative Extension. Reviewed May 2020. Accessed November 1, 2021. https://secure.caes.uga.edu/extension/publications/files/pdf/B%20 1318_5.PDF.

Perry, Leonard. "The Green Mountain Gardener." University of Vermont Extension. Accessed July 21, 2022. https://pss.uvm.edu/ppp/articleA.htm.

Perry, Leonard. "Perry's Perennial Pages." Department of Plant and Soil Science, University of Vermont. Accessed July 21, 2022. https://www.uvm.edu/~pass/perry/.

Riefner, Jr., Richard E. "*Ficus microcarpa* (Moraceae) Naturalized in Southern California, U.S.A.: Linking Plant, Pollinator, and Suitable Microhabitats to Document the Invasion Process." *Phytologia* 98, no. 1 (January 2016): 42–45. https://www.occnps.org/PDF/Ficusmicrocarpa-Riefner.pdf.

Royal Horticultural Society. "Find a Plant." RHS.org.uk. Accessed July 21, 2022. https://www.rhs.org.uk/plants/search-form.

Shapiro, Ari, and Arielle Pardes. "The Pink Congo Scam of Houseplant Influencer Instagram." *All Things Considered*, National Public Radio, February 20, 2020. Accessed November 19, 2021. https://www.npr.org/2020/02/20/807873782/the-pink-congo-scam-of-houseplant-influencer-instagram.

Toogood, Alan. *Plant Propagation*. New York: DK Publishing, 1999.

UConn Home and Garden Education Center. University of Connecticut Cooperative Extension System. Accessed July 21, 2022. http://www.ladybug.uconn.edu/.

University of Florida Gardening Solutions. Institute of Food and Agricultural Sciences Extension, University of Florida. Accessed July 21, 2022. https://gardeningsolutions.ifas.ufl.edu/.

University of Florida Institute of Food and Agricultural Sciences Extension, "Ask IFAS." University of Florida Electronic Data Information Source. Accessed July 21, 2022. https://edis.ifas.ufl.edu/.

University of Illinois Extension. "Herbs." University of Illinois Urbana-Champaign. Accessed July 21, 2022. https://web.extension.illinois.edu/herbs/.

University of Maryland Extension. "Nutrient Deficiency of Indoor Plants." Home and Garden Information Center, University of Maryland Extension. Accessed November 4, 2021. https://extension.umd.edu/resource/nutrient-deficiency-indoor-plants.

University of Minnesota Extension. "Yard and Garden." University of Minnesota Extension. Accessed July 21, 2022. https://extension.umn.edu/yard-and-garden.

University of Missouri Integrated Pest Management. "Environment and Garden." Division of Plant Sciences, University of Missouri. Accessed July 21, 2022. https://ipm.missouri.edu/MEG/.

Wisconsin Horticulture Division of Extension. "Articles." University of Wisconsin-Madison. Accessed July 21, 2022. https://hort.extension.wisc.edu/articles/.